The PEPPER
HARVEST COOKBOOK

The *The* PEPPER
HARVEST COOKBOOK

Barbara Ciletti

The Taunton Press

Taunton
BOOKS & VIDEOS
for fellow enthusiasts

Text © 1997 by Barbara Ciletti
Illustrations and photos by Boyd Hagen © 1997 by The Taunton Press

First printing: 1997
Printed in the United States of America

The Taunton Press, Inc., 63 South Main Street,
PO Box 5506, Newtown, CT 06470-5506
e-mail: tp@taunton.com

Library of Congress Cataloging-in-Publication Data

Ciletti, Barbara J.
    The pepper harvest cookbook / Barbara J. Ciletti.
        p.   cm.
    Includes bibliographical references and index.
    ISBN 1-56158-195-X
    1. Cookery (Peppers).   2. Peppers.   1. Title.
TX803.P46C55   1997   97-10086
  641.6'384 — dc21   CIP

ACKNOWLEDGMENTS

This cookbook came to life from the talent, encouragement, and commitment of many people. I hope that someday we may all come together to break bread and tell stories. Until that time, this page begins the process of sharing and thanks.

While I believe that writers don't necessarily require inspiration to put words to paper, composing the lyric of the kitchen requires a unique form of encouragement, wisdom, and freedom. When those elements come forth so generously from a publisher as fine as Helen Albert, an author works with creativity and facility. Yet, throughout every bookmaking process, challenges do occur, such as attempting to airfreight home-canned goods without breaking the seals or to import paprika from California to Colorado for grinding. Those moments gained levity and latitude because of Cherilyn DeVries.

Many thanks to my editor Diane Sinitsky for her equanimity and commitment to quality. Both show in this work. I'm grateful for the professional recipe testing by Connie Welch and for the pepper gallery check by the Pepper Gal, Betty Payton.

Thanks to photographer Tim Benko for photos that truly enhance the processing section. Thanks Tim, for your humor, creativity, and a vision that can even add life to canning utensils.

Of course photography would have been an academic excercise without the glistening chiles and bells that come from Susan Pope's farm in Wiggins, Colo. Cultivating a large cache of peppers is daunting to say the least. I grew as many as I could, but fortunately for me Pope Produce appeared without fail at the weekly farmer's market. Thanks, Susan, for your generous spirit, as well as the best produce I found all season.

Leonard and Carmela Ciletti unwittingly engendered the sense of celebration that awakens whenever I am in the kitchen. Leonard taught me the joy of learning and a strong appreciation for diversity and independence. I was always with my mother in the kitchen. Her encouragement fueled my imagination and taught me to challenge limits.

Each time I open this book I give thanks to my husband, Eric. He has contributed test shots, ideas, humor, and a true delight in sharing our recipes with a community of relatives and friends. His belief in me results in many achievements in and beyond our kitchen. He is, as my father would say, "the best."

CONTENTS

INTRODUCTION

As I think about peppers and the harvest, I draw from a wealth of expert information as well as from memories from my childhood. Vegetable gardens, orchards, and herbs were part of everyday life. My family took great pride in being as self-sufficient as possible. So once the summer solstice passed, we adopted an air of anticipation and low-key excitement. The days of digging, weeding, watering, and fertilizing yielded a bounty of food.

With the food came a buffet of celebrations. We converged with friends and family for myriad potlucks and a lively exchange of recipes and cultural traditions. We canned and froze food. We dried and blended herbs and spices. We made pies and pickles. And we filled dozens of pint jars for gifts, which I thought was the most appropriate act of all. I was taught that food was a gift from the earth, so sharing it meant gift giving to me. Although years have passed, we keep this celebration alive, whether we have friends at the supper table or can salsa for Christmas.

This book is meant to share the world of peppers and provide ways to create festivity as well as long-term yield from the harvest. The first part begins with a discussion of the Old World and New World legacy of this food, which is a vegetable as well as a spice. This part also includes facts about nutrition and flavor and talks of the cultural connections that come with the cultivation and harvest of different capsicums.

The gallery of peppers offers pictures and descriptions of 43 cultivars available in the United States. While this section is not meant to be all-inclusive, it gives the kitchen gardener or the cook who wants to use commercial produce practical information on physical characteristics, growing and harvesting, and flavor potential.

Although kitchen gardens appear to be reasonable enough in size as one orders seeds and plants, bumper crops occur on a regular basis, leaving the grower grasping for ways to either share or store the bounty. The harvesting and storing chapter offers tips for selecting produce, information on utensils, and methods for short-term and long-term storage. The next chapter offers advice on cooking peppers, including methods for roasting and stuffing.

The second part of this book consists of the recipes, which come from imagination and a desire to celebrate the freshness and flavor of the harvest. Ingredients, lore, and methods form the basis for an exchange of recipes from all over the world. A strong appreciation of the world community results from studying the methods, produce, climates, and traditions of different cultures.

Cookbooks are built from stories, be they fiction or nonfiction. This book evokes remembrance of a tale from August 1962. One late morning, my father and I were inspecting a large crop of peppers growing on some land that we had received use of for the summer. His friend Joe Consella was with us and was impressed by what promised to be a bumper crop of bells, wax peppers, and sweet bananas. He turned to my dad and said, "Leonard, what in the world are you going to do with all of these peppers? This crop is huge." My father stood still for a moment and then turned to face Joe with a patient, level gaze. "We'll eat 'em," he replied.

While that event took place years ago, its lesson still breathes today. This book is the result of my personal gardening experience and the opportunity to learn practical methods for harvesting and storing food from some great teachers. The recipes come from years of experimentation and research. I do hope that the recipes here pay proper respect to the great masters and mistresses of the kitchen—people like Diana Kennedy, whose understanding of the bond between a culture and its cuisine transforms food and all who eat it.

While this book is not all-inclusive, it does celebrate diversity, imagination, practicality, and the joy that transpires when the earth speaks and people listen.

THE WORLD OF PEPPERS

The pepper, known in every country and in nearly as many languages, offers a New World tale with origins steeped in Old World history. The pepper is indeed ancient, despite the fact that it is decidedly of the Americas and a resident of the New World. Its history and diversity have been the subjects of studies, stories, and theories. Such a fascination isn't too surprising for a little pod that grew wild for centuries before being tamed by the Indians in Peru and Mexico.

OLD AND NEW WORLD HISTORY

The genus *Capsicum* belongs to one of the largest and earliest families of the plant kingdom, the *Solanaceae*. Research shows that flowering plants and trees, along with dinosaurs and mammals, emerged during the Cenozoic Era, which began about 60 million years ago. By comparison, modern man has existed for at least 40,000 years, while agriculture started about 11,000 years ago. Archeological records tell us that people were probably eating wild peppers as early as 7000 B.C. and that they finally began domesticating the peppers between 5200 B.C. and 3400 B.C. While the actual date of domestication isn't exact, researchers in Chicama Valley in Peru uncovered a batch of preserved peppers that dates back to 2500 B.C., indicating that the South Americans were possibly eating and growing the ají, which is their name for chile.

The wild pepper was then, and remains today, a perennial in tropical climates. The pepper's remarkable diversity arose from a stable climate, along with pollination aided by the wind, insects, and even birds. Those compact, leafy plants probably came equipped with a built-in method of seed dispersal, whereby the pods were easily loosened, allowing capsicums to grow in profusion. The plants bore green pods that the ancient humans ate fresh as a vegetable and dried for use as a spice.

Cultivation

The domestication of the pepper came about with the development of agriculture and the taming of animals. The hunters and gatherers were beginning to eat more

plants as hunting became less profitable. Changes in climate and dramatic shifts in the earth's evolution, along with hunting, led to the decrease and in some cases extinction of herds.

New vs. Old World methods

The need to survive forced humans to plan for the future and harness the wild. The New World inhabitants developed agricultural methods that differed from those used in the Old World. Old World people gathered seeds and flung them far and wild over the fields, which is similar to pollination by the wind. However, New World farmers took the time to be more deliberate, thus planting the seeds in the earth. This made sense for the pre-Columbian farmer because more than half of his daily diet consisted of plants. Survival couldn't be left to chance.

In the Old World, plants were harvested once the pods were fully matured, but various New World plants, including the capsicum, were eaten at different stages of growth. The maturity of the fruit probably dictated to some degree the intended culinary use. In addition, many Old World crops had sturdy root systems, but the New World plants did not. Thus, the New World farmer had to keep a more watchful eye over the growing process.

Taming the wild pepper

Taming and training the wild pepper began its process of adaptation and change. The wild peppers were more than likely small, round, conical, or slightly elongated pods, some of which were no more than an inch or two in length, that grew erect. They fell easily from their calyxes, the green, leafy caps that issue forth the fruit, which made them easy to pluck, as birds and humans would discover.

The pods' color, no doubt, caught the eyes of birds, who made the pods a mainstay in their diet. The birds plucked the pods, ate them, and digested them. The seeds then returned to the earth as fertilizer, having passed through the birds' digestive tracts intact. The seeds grew into plants.

Farmers began devising ways to help their crops reach maturity without being ravaged by birds. One method was to bend the stems of the plants, thus hiding the pods under leaves. As pods began to grow in pendant fashion, they couldn't be seen and therefore stolen by birds.

As growers became more knowledgeable about agricultural methods, the capsicum changed dramatically in color, size, flavor, and shape. Thus began the processes that engendered diversification far beyond, perhaps, what would have occurred had man not been in the picture.

Trade routes and travel

As man became more sophisticated in agriculture, the world was also harnessing animals, developing a more complex social structure, and traversing the seas. With travel came an exchange of customs and goods, including spices.

BLACK PEPPER

Despite the capsicum's common name of "pepper," it is not related to black pepper, or *Piper nigrum*. Capsicums are pods, while black peppercorns are berries. The capsicum may have been labeled "pepper" by the Europeans because the ground dried chile has similar spice characteristics as black pepper.

Black pepper, which is native to India's Malabar Coast, is not a bush but a climbing vine, which can extend to 20 ft. without cultivation. The vine's dark, heart-shaped leaves surround clusters of green berries that later turn red. The berries yield the best flavor when harvested just as they begin to get a reddish hue. Once picked and dried, they turn black and wrinkled. Both black and white peppercorns come from the same fruit. White peppercorns are simply harvested berries with the skin rubbed off.

According to Theophrastus in 33 B.C., the Romans and Greeks used black pepper as a medicine as well as a condiment. With the opening of trade routes to the Orient centuries later, black pepper became probably the most popular trade item. Consequently, cultivation of pepper plants spread throughout the world. Today, black pepper is one of the most universal seasonings.

The Arabs embraced a cache of herbs and spices used for cooking at a time when the rest of the known world ate rather simple, unadorned food. The Greeks and Romans probably received their first taste of ground black pepper, cardamom, or any number of pungent culinary devices from the Arabs, who came to call by way of Egypt, a country known even then for exotic cuisine.

These spices remained a pretty well-kept secret until Marco Polo developed trade routes to the Orient in the 13th century. His quest for spices, of which black pepper was considered the gem, spanned more than two decades. His repeated journeys, combined with a sharing of goods and customs, created a bridge between cultures.

However, it was the Italian explorer Christopher Columbus, who in search of one kind of pepper introduced the world to another. Columbus considered himself a failure for never fulfilling his quest of finding a shorter

route to the Far East for Spain's Ferdinand and Isabella. But his landing in the New World led explorers to new discoveries that changed the way people began to think about food and medicine.

One of those discoveries was the capsicum. When the Spanish invaded the New World, they found at least four different pepper species growing under the auspices of developed agricultural methods. As trade routes developed over land and sea from 1493 on, the explorers carried the pepper pods and seeds all over the Americas and on a rather circuitous route back to Europe.

The Portuguese had obtained the capsicum around the beginning of the 1500s. Portuguese explorers carried pepper with them as they sailed around the Cape of Good Hope, thereby introducing it to Africa, and to the Far East, which included their first journey to India. The Turkish onslaught on Portugal in 1513 brought the Turks the rich, red paprika pod, the spice that would revolutionize Hungarian

BIRDS AND BELLS

When Columbus arrived at the shores of Central America, he found that the Indians there had been cultivating peppers productively for years. While the exact origin of when the bell pepper received its name is subject to mystery, we know that Lionel Wafer, a British surgeon and pirate, used the name as early as 1681.

The Indians of Panama offered Wafer refuge after he was wounded in a gunpowder explosion and abandoned by his comrades. The Indians treated his wounds and offered friendship and, of course, food. Wafer later wrote about his experiences and said that the Indians ate two different cultivars of peppers in great quantities. One was called the bell pepper, presumably because of its shape. The other was the bird pepper, the name the Indians gave the chiltepin variety because the birds had a fondness for eating them.

and eventually all Slavic cuisine. The Italians had the capsicum by 1535, with Germany following in 1542 and Moravia in 1585.

Certainly thousands of years had passed since the capsicum first underwent domestication, but its popularity grew quickly after its discovery by the Europeans. The pepper gained much attention because of its incredible diversity.

As pepper fascination spread, people began writing down their thoughts. Today we benefit from histories, testimonials, and diaries that extoll the capsicum and describe the customs and culture of peoples observed by the Europeans. For instance, from 1547 to 1555, the Hessian Hans Stade spent his days in eastern Brazil as a captive of the Indians. He concluded that America grew two types of peppers: red ones and yellow ones. He also wrote that when the pepper was in its green or immature state, it "was about the size of a haw, from a hawthorne bush." He went on to say that the peppers, regardless of their size or growth, were very, very hot. The Indians ate them daily and dried them in the sun for future use.

An Englishman named Edward Long lived on the island of Jamaica during the 18th century, making a career of cultivating a plantation and writing history. He found 15 well-established types of peppers there that were being used fresh, dried, and for pickling. I wouldn't have initially thought that little Jamaica would have been prolific in pepper production, but back then, the island was a queen of ports and right in the path of a burgeoning line of sea traffic.

Dried paprikas are among several cultivars that have been loved as a spice for centuries.

PEPPERS AS FOOD

Certainly, the capsicum has undergone continuous rounds of evolution and discovery. It is a well-traveled plant, whose diversity and popularity have survived thousands of earth years. Peppers belong to the esteemed *Solanaceae* family of the plant kingdom. This family, also called the nightshade family, encompasses tomatoes, eggplant, potatoes, and tobacco as well.

The genus *Capsicum* contains five domesticated species (see the chart at right). These species house all other domesticated capsicums, including the 43 cultivars discussed in this book.

Regardless of the many specific differences among cultivars, capsicums as a group have a reputation for intense and often bright color, unmistakable pungency and aroma, and, to many, an unforgettable flavor. All result from a special balance of chemicals, which are romanced by the sun, nurtured by the soil, and quenched by water.

As food, the pepper offers a host of uses. When eaten raw or cooked, it provides energy and immunity to disease. Whether hot, mild, or pungently sweet, the pepper offers diversity in the kitchen. Besides being edible as a vegetable by itself, the pepper adds flavor and nutrients to appetizers, soups, main dishes, and

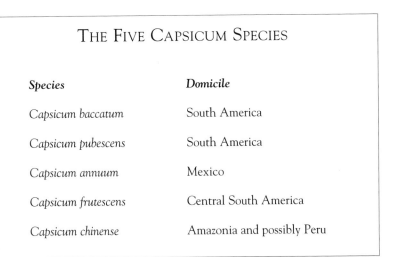

THE FIVE CAPSICUM SPECIES

Species	Domicile
Capsicum baccatum	South America
Capsicum pubescens	South America
Capsicum annuum	Mexico
Capsicum frutescens	Central South America
Capsicum chinense	Amazonia and possibly Peru

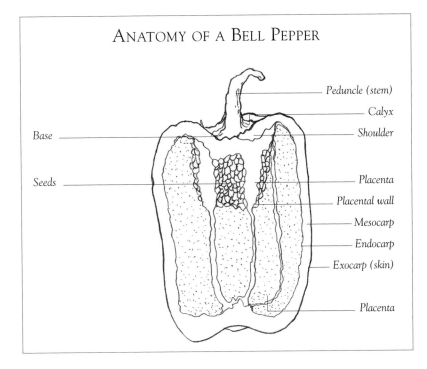

ANATOMY OF A BELL PEPPER

Base

Seeds

Peduncle (stem)

Calyx

Shoulder

Placenta

Placental wall

Mesocarp

Endocarp

Exocarp (skin)

Placenta

condiments. The pepper's journey throughout the New and Old Worlds has led to its proliferation, as well as to dishes that reflect the cultures of various ethnic groups. Consequently, it's no surprise that hot and sweet peppers reside in a place of esteem among many peoples of the earth, including Americans, Thais, Italians, Asians, Mexicans, and Hungarians.

The well-traveled pepper engenders appreciation for the mores and culinary methods in kitchens the world over. The influences remain subtle yet binding as we all share the ingredients, flavors, and methods commanded by various ethnic recipes. As we think about the cayenne, jalapeño, cubanelle, or tabasco pepper, we make powerful connections with people who lived long before us and others we will never see.

As I read stories about paella, I came to truly appreciate that it, as well as many other dishes I have either read about, made, or even taken for granted, is not a main dish but a cultural event. This educational process happened over and over again, as I studied the ingredients for curry, searched for the balance in pizza sauce, or blended the aïoli.

Perhaps one of the most important roles of peppers is their influence on cooking, which has connected people from all over the world. Throughout history, peppers have been discovered by a particular culture, which was, in turn, changed as it expanded its understanding and appreciation of vegetables and spices.

Flavor and aroma

Whether sweet or hot, peppers offer a complex and nutritious combination of flavors that are directly related to their colors. The level of chemicals found in carotenoid pigments seem to determine how much flavor a pepper will offer. Peppers that are plump and bright, almost glossy with color, abound with flavor. As color pales, for instance, in dried peppers, the flavor diminishes. But don't think that the flavor disappears; it simply mellows.

Peppers contain such a delightful array of aromas that you would think the scents were somehow sent to accompany the equally broad palette of oranges, reds, greens, purples, golden yellows, and pale, creamy lilacs. The pasilla resonates with a delicate raisin aroma that matches the reddish-brown wrinkles on its dried skin. (Since pasilla means raisin in Spanish, the texture and scent of this pepper complement its nomenclature perfectly.) The mirasol gleams with cherry red flesh

POBLANOS VS. ANCHOS

When poblanos or fresh mulatos are dried, they are called anchos. Of course, poblanos and anchos have different uses. Poblanos are great for roasting and stuffing, while anchos are typically ground and used in sauces and salsas. Anchos make a wonderful ingredient for mole, a spicy Mexican sauce usually served with poultry.

Cooking with the poblano and ancho is fun, but knowing how to select a quality pepper takes practice. Reporter Amal Naj once shared the perfect description of the perfect poblano: "It can't be even a bit wrinkly. Poblanos have to be like a baby's bottom. No wrinkles, no brown spots."

Poblanos vary in Scoville units (see p. 38). The lighter green chiles can be pretty mild, while the darker ones, especially those taking on a little red, can be very hot. However, you can't really tell how hot the chile is until you take a bite of it. Some of the darker peppers can be mild, while others will produce steam out your ears. The ancho also varies in heat.

and entices the chili lover with the whimsical yet light scent of strawberries. Golden bells bless the nostrils with a combination of lemon piquantness and a hint of clove and spice. Incidentally, bell peppers contain the chemical flavor compound that produces the lovely bouquet found in Cabernet Sauvignon.

Nutrition
The pepper contains significant levels of vitamins C, A, E, and B. In fact, peppers can have more than six times the amount of vitamin C found in oranges, according to Rebecca Rupp in *Blue Corn and Square Tomatoes*.

Raw peppers offer the best result for those wanting to supplement their diet with vitamin C. However, even though vitamin C is sensitive to heat, peppers lose only about 30 percent of their vitamin C content when baked or canned.

Peppers outdistance carrots in the amount of vitamin A and do not lose any of the vitamin's content through cooking. So, peppers are also good for those who want to nurture their eyes.

In addition, capsicums are also high in vitamin B, offering all members of that particular complex. Vitamin B feeds the nervous system and the brain, keeping us calm and alert. The combination of vitamins, capsaicin, which aids digestion, and chlorophyll, which cleanses the bloodstream, makes peppers a truly healthy food.

PEPPERS AS MEDICINE
In the New World, the pepper was appreciated as a food and a healing agent, long before the Europeans began to understand and use it as such. Recently, studies have shown that the pepper's vitamin C contributes to good health, while the clear, odorless, tasteless chemical capsaicin literally kills bacteria.

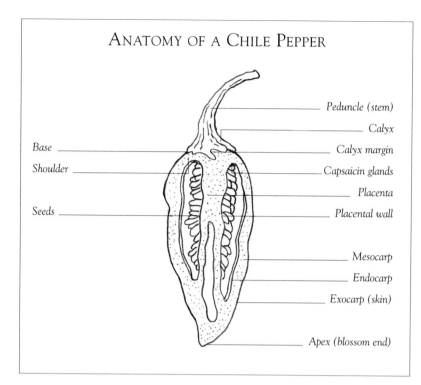

ANATOMY OF A CHILE PEPPER

Peduncle (stem)
Calyx
Base
Calyx margin
Shoulder
Capsaicin glands
Placenta
Seeds
Placental wall

Mesocarp
Endocarp
Exocarp (skin)

Apex (blossom end)

But not all peppers have therapeutic potential. It is the chile, which contains capsaicin, not the sweet pepper, that will cure a lot of what ails you. Capsaicin's ability to numb certain active neurons has a deadening effect on some bacteria, resulting in pain relief and the eventual demise of body-harming germs. Over the centuries, the chile has been used to alleviate gout, smallpox, dysentery, and even bubonic plague. It is an excellent antiseptic on open cuts and is effective for stopping profuse bleeding.

In addition, chiles aid the digestive system by increasing the production of stomach acid, the major agent in the digestive process. It stimulates the digestive tract, eliminating everything that the body doesn't really need. This cleansing process can be critical in countries where the diet is somewhat bland or high in fats and carbohydrates. Chiles, especially cayenne, speed up the metabolism and burn off molecules that literally weigh you down. However, this is not a suggestion to overuse chiles for weight loss, which seems to be a recent and popular recommendation. Like everything else, balance and moderation play a key role in the diet, health, and longevity of the human body.

Chiles can also offer external relief as part of a topical agent. Capsaicin cream has been respected for years as a pain reliever for arthritis, rheumatism, surgical scars, toothaches, and even migraines. The cream needs to be applied lightly several times a day. Since the ingredients for homemade cream can vary, along with its intensity and required dosage, consult a reliable source before attempting to create a concoction meant as a cure.

The heat factor

Frequently called the bite that bites back, the chile has been loved, sought, and sometimes avoided for its sting. Capsaicin literally brings tears to the eyes of the uneducated, albeit enthusiastic, adventurer rambling about in the kingdom of chiles. This fire remains at bay within glands nestled just under the base and shoulder and in the veins along the inner wall (see the drawing on the facing page).

It's best to check into the heat factor or Scoville units of specific varieties before touching and tasting them (see p. 38). That lovely green or orange little pod can literally take your breath away, as well as a few cells of skin. Capsaicin is an irritant that remains insoluble in water, so calling the fire department does no good. Hotter chiles simply need to be respected; they should be handled with caution and eaten with care. Since capsaicin has a tantalizing yet numbing effect, it's not surprising that early con-sumers of the chile led some observers to question the consumers' mental stability. It's said that Aztecs would combine cold chocolate with chile for a morning pick-me-up. Interestingly, capsaicin offers a double punch: After one survives the pain of eating a chile, a pleasant reverie follows, as the brain releases the endorphins that counter anxiety and promote good moods. Certainly that overall good feeling, or high,

THE TABASCO PEPPER

Sometime during the mid-1800s, the spicy tabasco pepper was brought to Louisiana from Mexico. Tabasco plantations spread throughout the southern tip of the state, as well as to Avery Island, one of five islands off the Louisiana coast that literally sits atop a dome of salt.

The years preceding and following the Civil War played a crucial role in the germination of what is now a global industry. In 1865, Edmund McIlhenny returned to the Avery Island plantation he fled amidst the Union invasion of 1863. While most of the family plantation had been ruined, the land yielded a few survivors. McIlhenny harvested what tabascos he could, crushed them, added salt, and let the mash set in crockery jars. After a process of fermentation, stirring, and more fermentation, he strained the mixture and poured the liquid into cologne bottles. By 1868, McIlhenny not only added a delightful piquancy to the diet of his friends and neighbors, but also created public demand for his sauce. Tabasco sauce was on its way to becoming a business that spanned the globe.

About 25 years ago, the Louisiana plantations began to disappear, with acres of plants succumbing to various diseases. Many plantation owners gave up because of bankruptcy, frustration, or both. As labor costs increased, still more farmers refused to continue in what was already a labor-intensive project.

Today Avery Island remains as the last bastion of tabasco plantations. Here the McIlhenny Company still cultivates this pepper for its Tabasco sauce. Yet Louisiana yields peppers from just 230 acres, which account for less than 10 percent of the pepper's demand. To meet the remaining demand, the company has contracts with farmers in Mexico, Venezuela, Honduras, and Colombia, where nature and economic conditions are kinder to the harvest.

Edmund McIlhenny's sauce has traveled far beyond the boundaries of that little island. Enhancing the tables of people all over the world, the sauce adds a little spice to Cajun cuisine while lending a glimpse at the culture of the Louisiana people.

THE PEPPER-EATING CONTEST

When I was growing up, my parents would take me and my brothers to visit our relatives nearly every Sunday. Dinner, which was held at midday, contained the usual rounds of soup, pasta, chicken, bread, salad, and a tray of mixed olives, sharp cheese, pickled peppers, and roasted peppers. That tray was the only dish that was put on the table at the beginning of the meal and removed empty at the conclusion of it.

One Sunday afternoon, after the table had been cleared and the adults left us to our own devices, an interesting challenge occurred. My cousin, who was 14, boasted that he could eat more hot peppers than any of the 12 cousins sitting at the table. I was 9 years old.

"Is that so?" I asked.

"Yes," he replied.

I challenged him to a contest. The first person to finish a pint of hot cherry peppers and garlic would win and become the undisputed "Great Respected One."

He laughed at me. So did my brothers and other cousins. He outweighed me by at least 40 pounds. But it wasn't capacity that would win the contest. It was defiance. The contest began. I succeeded in holding my breath for a while—long enough to get four or five peppers down. Then I would breathe carefully, being sure that I didn't take in too much air. The more air, the greater the pain (I had been prac-

ticing for months). Meanwhile, my cousin tried to bite the peppers in half or eat them whole. His face got red and the tips of his ears turned bright pink. He couldn't get through his pint. I continued to eat, albeit quickly, until the last cherry pepper was gone. I immediately reached for a piece of bread, ate it, and exhaled. I won the contest and became the "Great Respected One," until we established a pistachio-eating contest two weeks later. Fame, regardless of how it is attained, can often be short-lived.

To this day, I don't know how I ate those peppers, and neither does my cousin. Yes, I won the contest, but I remained physically altered for days.

THE PSYCHOLOGY OF EATING PEPPERS

According to Rebecca Rupp in *Blue Corn and Square Tomatoes*, psychologist Paul Rozin contends that eating hot peppers, like watching horror films, contains an element of constrained risk. The body responds with warning signals, such as burning eyes, sweat, and a hot palate, but the situation is not really dangerous. Even so, if I had to choose between eating a single raw habanero or watching a film about body snatchers, I'd probably choose the film.

can be produced through intense exercise. However, disciples of the chile may attest that eating peppers can be a whole lot more fun than working out at the gym.

Yet, the very chemical that excites the palate has also been known as strong medicine for breaking certain habits. Aztec and Inca

mothers would rub chile on their nipples when weaning their babies. Today, capsaicin is used as a spray to keep unwanted pets away from certain areas and even to discourage fights in New York subways. Whatever the use, the chile and its powerhouse of pleasure and pain should be respected and used with caution.

A GALLERY OF PEPPERS

Capsicums come in more than 500 varieties with a wide range of sizes and colors. Their flavors and uses provide a highly diversified world for the gardener and cook. While the many varieties offer intrigue, this gallery is meant to discuss peppers that are readily available, feasible to grow, and practical for the kitchen. You'll find sweet, hot, and heirloom varieties to add color to the garden and nutrients to different foods.

ETHNIC AND HEIRLOOM PEPPERS

While we know that all peppers had to originate somewhere, certain cultivars possess a flavor that suggest a distinct ethnic flair. A dish of rellenos made with roasted Joe Parker chiles sends the senses off to Albuquerque or Santa Fe. Roasted figaros served with rosemary focaccia and a glass of Chianti make me wish I was in Tuscany again, while my friend and fellow cook Chee refuses to stir-fry without Thai hots.

Over the years, some Old World cultivars gradually disappeared with the immigrants who brought them to this country. These cultivars were replaced by less specialized pepper varieties that became more widely accepted as the second and third generations of families adapted to America. Today, the diligence and research of a number of dedicated growers allow us to once again experience a few of these tasty "heirlooms." A little research and time spent shopping through seed catalogs could yield palate-pleasing results well worth your effort.

Banana (C. annuum)

These peppers are long and shiny, with a shape and color much like the fruit they were named for. Most grow 2 in. across and taper up to 8 in. long. Probably originating in Hungary, they can be sweet or hot. Although they are usually picked before they fully develop, banana peppers transform from yellow to a warm, intense scarlet hue when mature. Both the sweet and hot varieties grow well in hot, sunny climates with plenty of loose, well-fed, weed-free soil.

Banana

Bulgarian carrot

Banana peppers do not dry well and are best used fresh. Sweet, yellow Hungarian banana peppers are outstanding in goulash, sauces, and stews. Sweet bananas are also good for sauces and in combination with tomatoes, onions, summer squash, and eggplant. They're particularly good when fried, then packed with salt, garlic, and virgin olive oil. This mixture can be canned or kept for up to three weeks in the refrigerator. Banana peppers freeze easily, needing no blanching prior to storage.

Sweet banana peppers of any ethnic origin tend to be thin-skinned with fleshy walls that are crunchy and easy to bite into. When cut in half lengthwise and stuffed with various fillings of cheese, herbs, and seafood, these peppers can be served as an appetizer or as a side to salads and main dishes.

Banana varieties such as hot Hungarian wax peppers turn from yellow to sunset shades of fiery orange that deepen to red when ripe. They peel easily after roasting, which enhances their flavor and volume. These peppers make a delicious and pungent main dish when stuffed and baked. They also make a sweet and savory condiment when canned with olive oil, garlic, and orange slices.

Bulgarian carrot (C. annuum)

These bright orange, fiery heirloom chiles grow to 3½ in. long and are shaped like a carrot. They grow best in temperatures between 70°F to 75°F with the plants spaced 16 in. to 18 in. apart in rich soil. This cultivar has stocky seedlings with well-developed roots that produce vigorous foliage and fruit when heavily mulched and fed. These chiles thrive when watered frequently, but require good drainage. While many peppers can be harvested when green, these should remain on their plants until they reach a shiny, full, hot-looking orange.

Bulgarian carrot chiles are not only hot but fruity. This combination makes for tasty, chunky chutneys and tangy marinades for beef, pork, poultry, and shellfish. They lend a little snap to pickles, salsas, sauces, rice, and potatoes. Since these chiles require more water for growing than most, they also hold more and don't dry well. They're best when added to preserves, jams, and relishes.

Cadice (C. annuum)

Cadice peppers are extra-early French hybrids, best for growing in short-season areas. They also thrive in cooler climates that can be marginal for other cultivars. These plants will grace your garden with abundant fruit that may turn from green to red faster than any other pepper you may grow. They're also some of the earliest bell-type peppers available at produce markets.

Cadice begin to yield fruit 55 days after planting and continue to offer plenty more for three to five weeks. These bushy yet compact plants grow well in gardens as well as in containers.

Cadice are sweet, big, and crunchy with firm, fleshy walls. Their glossy green or deep red stages of development certainly brighten up any garden. Peppers at either stage are delicious eaten raw in salads, and they freeze well without blanching first. They also make an interesting flavor combination when cooked with a more pungent pepper, onions, and tomatoes. Try the sweet cadice as a perfect blend with the mild heat of an Anaheim chile.

Corno di toro (C. annuum)

These heirloom Italian peppers bear fruit 8 in. to 10 in. long and grow best in warm soil once outside temperatures exceed 65°F. These plants like plenty of sun and need to be spaced 18 in. to 24 in. apart. They also need plenty of water, mulch, and a weed-free environment.

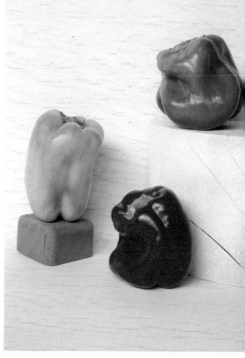

Cadice

Corno di toro

Well-fed and well-watered corno plants offer long branches that need to be staked because of the weight of their fruit. When harvesting, cut (don't pull) the pepper from the plant once green fruit matures to a glossy yellow or red. As with most pepper plants, picking fruit stimulates productivity. This pepper, called "horn of a bull," looks more like a red or yellow cone when fully ripe.

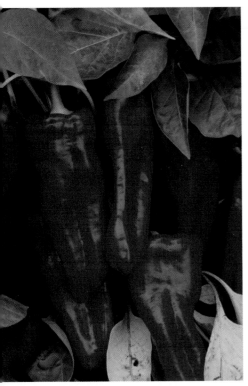

Cubanelle

Since the walls of the corno are firm with delicate flesh, these peppers are perfect for salads and grilling. Or leave some whole and gently sauté a batch in a cast-iron skillet that contains ½ cup of extra-virgin olive oil and three or four mashed cloves of garlic. My grandmother used to serve a platter of these sautéed peppers with tomato and basil salad, dry provolone or mozzarella cheese, and thick, toasted slices of crusty bread. We would rub the bread into the oil on the platter, then place the cheese on the bread. We would pick up the peppers by their stems and aim for the mouth. Finally, the tomatoes cleared the palate.

Cornos are good raw but better sautéed or roasted. They enhance tomato sauces, pasta, eggs, and other vegetables such as mushrooms, onions, and zucchini. They store well when canned with garlic, lemon, and tomatoes. Use them fresh or bag them for the freezer.

Cubanelle (C. annuum)
Cubanelles are gaining popularity with growers and cooks throughout North America. Although these peppers are considered Italian in origin, varieties such as the sweet Hungarian, gypsy, and Romanian also claim identity as cubanelles. The peppers mature in 65 to 70 days and display vibrant hues of gold, flame orange, and red. Cubanelles are sweet yet mildly pungent. They've become a favorite of those who enjoy peppers fried or sautéed whole or in slices.

Figaro (C. annuum)
These Italian heirloom pimientos remind me of tiny pumpkins. They're round and slightly flattened at the top and bottom. Figaros grow well with plenty of water and sun. After 68 days of cultivation, these strong plants yield an abundance of emerald green peppers that turn to a warm, deep red at maturity. I have found them to be one of the easiest peppers to grow during a short season. They need warm but not hot nights and loose soil.

Most people think of pimientos as a stuffing for olives or as a condiment found in tiny jars on the grocer's shelf. However,

Figaro

Italian sweet hybrid

they're some of the best peppers to eat raw by themselves, in salads, or on sandwiches. Their smooth skin covers walls of thick, sweet, crunchy flesh. My father always said that eating figaros was better than eating candy, and he had quite a sweet tooth.

These peppers are better canned than frozen. They should be eaten fresh or processed in jars with peppercorns, garlic, and vinegar. Figaros also enhance caponata, eggplant, olives, and mushrooms.

Italian sweet hybrid (C. annuum)

These are one of the classic staples in the Italian kitchen. The plants grow well with plenty of sun and well-drained and well-fed soil. These hybrids are high-yield, slightly bushy plants that begin to offer fruit for picking after 70 days. The peppers are 6 in. to 8 in. long, with thin, smooth skin. Their green flesh has a bit more carotene than other pepper varieties, so every pepper sports a touch of red on a side or where it tapers toward the end.

Italian hybrids are usually homegrown or available during the summer and early fall at produce markets. Slightly pungent but not hot, these peppers are good in salads, on the grill, stir-fried, or sautéed whole. When I was a child, my family would make pepper sandwiches. We would patiently wait until the peppers were cool enough to touch and then pull out the stem and seeds. Three or four peppers between two pieces of fresh bread created a reward well worth the effort. These peppers also add a snap to pork, sausage, and tomatoes. They make a zesty tomato sauce for sausage and peppers and pizza.

Kolasca sweet spice paprika

Kolasca sweet spice paprika (C. annuum)

Kolasca is an authentic Hungarian cultivar and one of the paprikas that has given its homeland a reputation for fine, complex cuisine with a unique sweet-hot balance. These peppers need full sun and rich, mulched soil. When planted 2 ft. apart, watered regularly, and kept free from weeds, they thrive. These paprikas are best when harvested once they have grown to 1½ in.

across by 5 in. long. Their shiny, brilliant red color indicates that they have fully matured and are at their peak of flavor.

These peppers aren't to be eaten raw or cooked; kolascas should be dried the same way as other chiles. Most people don't think of paprika as a chile, but its hauntingly sweet yet quiet flavor also includes an ever-so-slightly pungent redolence. There's nothing quite like a cache of home-made paprika.

Kolascas are considered by many to be the best Eastern European paprikas available. Their flat, thin-walled fruit can be strung into ristras (see pp. 46-48) and dried indoors of you live in a mild climate. Or the whole plant can be pulled from the ground and hung to dry if you live in a hotter, drier climate.

Petite Sirah (C. annuum)

These mild, conical-shaped peppers are perfect for pints of sweet pickles. The fruits grow to 2 in. to 2½ in. long and about 1 in. wide at the

Petite Sirah

top, and taper to a point. Growing to 24 in. in height, the plants yield fruit prolifically after 65 to 70 days. Blossoms yield light, lemony-colored fruits that ripen to a deep, crisp red. I enjoy these peppers raw with a little lemon, basil, parsley, and lemon thyme or pickled with just enough lemon and vinegar to enhance the flavor of cloves and other spices. They store well dried in the pantry for months.

Thai hot dragon hybrid (C. chinense)

Thai hot dragon hybrids are among the hottest peppers in the world. These peppers are so hot that they are usually added to stir-fry and other Asian dishes for flavor but then removed. Having more than about eight times the heat of jalapeños, these are too hot for most people to even attempt to consume.

These chile plants grow to about 2 ft. high and offer a very heavy yield, with one plant producing up to 200 fruits. The deep green peppers ripen to deep red fruits that dry easily. Thais grow to 3 in. to 4 in. long and ½ in. wide at the top, and taper to a rounded point.

BELL PEPPERS

The bell was first addressed by British buccaneer Lionel Wafer in 1681, when he saw its cultivation in Panama. We're pretty certain that, like many plants, its name describes the shape of its fruit. That name has been with us ever since and represents about 83 cultivars growing throughout the

Thai hot dragon hybrid

world today. These cultivars can grow erect or pendant with as little as two but no more than four lobes. Bells can be green, yellow, orange, red, violet, purple, chocolate, and even ivory in color. They are suitable for eating raw, chopping or slicing for the freezer, or cooking into sauces for canning. Each variety has its own flavor. Some, like the French vidi, are sweet yet mild and succulent. Others, such as the

Yankee bell, pack a bit more zest when they're green and become sweeter as they mature to red. Experiment with different cultivars and mix flavors and colors from sweet to spicy, from green to yellow, orange, red, and purple. They're all worth a try.

The following pages list some of the more popular bells, with information about maturity, flavor, and uses.

Ace

Ariane

Ace (C. annuum)

Aces are vigorous and highly productive, with nearly every flower producing a pepper. Fruit appears about 50 days after young plants are transplanted in the garden, thus they're one of the first peppers to appear at the market in the summer. Because they are hardy, aces are highly successful for gardeners who otherwise may not have much luck growing peppers. The plants yield small and medium, three- and four-lobed, green glossy fruit.

Ariane (C. annuum)

Arianes claim Holland as their country of origin and yield fruit about 68 days after planting outdoors. These are big, blocky bells that turn from green to a glowing, vibrant orange when mature. Their thick, crunchy flesh offers a sweet, zesty flavor as rich as their color. Arianes are sumptuous raw, stir-fried, or baked.

Bell tower (C. annuum)

These large, thick-walled peppers offer a zesty yet mild flavor. They are three- or four-lobed, boxy peppers that ripen from green to a bright red. Gardeners in all but very short-season growing regions can produce fairly prolific plants that yield fruit at about 70 days. Bell towers are also resistant to the plant virus tobacco mosaic.

Bell tower

California wonder

Big Bertha

Cooks enjoy these peppers because of their many uses. They make crunchy, pungent yet sweet additions to salads. They don't fall apart in casseroles, and they keep their shape and body for stuffed peppers. These peppers freeze well.

Big Bertha (C. annuum)

These giant, sweet, green bells are favorites at farmer's markets as well as in the kitchen garden. These peppers can be as wide as 4 in. and as long as 7 in. They add a tangy flavor to salads and stir-fry. Plants are sturdy and grow to a fairly bushy height of 24 in. to 30 in. They begin to yield fruit after 65 to 70 days, requiring a fairly temperate climate, well-drained soil, and plenty of sun.

California wonder (C. annuum)

These peppers were introduced to American gardens in 1928 and now account for several thousand pounds of peppers that come out of California every year. These peppers are big, blocky, sweet, and perfect for stuffing and in salads. The fruits turn from bright green to brilliant, glossy red when mature. They also freeze well.

Chocolate beauty

Corona

Chocolate beauty (C. annuum)

Chocolate beauties offer visual contrast to the lively mix of green, yellow, and red bells during harvest time. These medium-sized, blocky peppers begin as green, then ripen to a warm, slightly reddish chocolate shade. Inside are walls of sweet, red flesh. If you want to grow your own, you won't be disappointed: These vigorous plants yield plenty of peppers for the table as well as for storage.

Corona (C. annuum)

These bells begin green and ripen to a glowing orange color. These sweet peppers freeze well and add color to salads and pastas. They gain a little volume when pan or oven roasted and also keep their body in soups and sauces.

The plants are small and compact, producing medium-sized, squat bells after 65 to 70 days. The plants, which need well-watered and well-drained soil, resist tobacco mosaic.

Golden bell (C. annuum)

Golden bells, otherwise called quadrato d'oro, display fruit with the four golden lobes that evoked their name. Thick, juicy walls of sweet flesh make them perfect for eating raw and for cooking in casseroles, sauces, and a variety of ethnic dishes. Golden bells will fill your kitchen with a sweet, slightly cloved scent. The peppers combine well with a variety of sweet and savory herbs and spices, such as basil, oregano, garlic, cinnamon, clove, and fennel.

Gypsy hybrid
(C. annuum)

These tapered, sweet peppers are hybrids that ripen from green to flaming shades of yellow, orange, and red. These peppers freeze and pickle well and are also excellent for frying. They can be hot packed with olive oil, garlic, herbs, and spices for enjoyment throughout the winter. Yielding fruit after 60 to 65 days, the plants require temperate nights, well-drained, fertilized soil, and sunny days. They also resist tobacco mosaic.

Ivory charm (C. annuum)

A bite of the ivory charm tastes like a bite of a sweet green bell. However, these peppers begin white in color, instead of green. The fruit ripens from a creamy, soft hue to a soft, gentle yellow destined to delight the eye. The peppers are attractive ornamentals, but they are edible as well. They are typically used in salads.

Golden bell

Gypsy hybrid

Ivory charm

Lilac bell

These peppers are excellent raw in salads, with dips, or with aïoli. They also freeze well and lend a fruity zest to dishes that ordinarily call for bell peppers.

The plants are reliable producers and are naturally resistant to a variety of viruses. They bush out, growing leafy canopies that support and shelter the fruits. These peppers are both colorful and fun to grow. Because I never thought about seeing peppers with lavender skin until recently, they reminded me of a rhyme from my childhood: "Have you ever seen a purple cow?…"

Northstar (C. annuum)

These bells are favorites among growers in northern climates where the soil and temperature conditions can be somewhat unforgiving. The peppers yield in 59 to 65 days, creating options for gardeners with very short growing seasons. Introduced about five or six years ago, these plants produce medium-sized, thick-walled fruits that are delicious raw and freeze well. The three-

Plants yield prolifically after 65 to 70 days, continuing to bear fruit throughout the summer. They resist sunburn, respond well to watered, well-drained soil, and withstand a variety of viruses.

Lilac bell (C. annuum)

These hybrids, like ivory charms, carry the flavor of green bells without growing through a green stage. These fruits mature from a light lavender to a rich, deep lavender to a deep, fruity red.

Northstar

Orobelle

Pepperoncini

or four-lobed, crisp, zesty peppers begin green and ripen to red.

Orobelle (C. annuum)

These glowing, deeply rich, yellow peppers are frequently dubbed the best of the golden bells. The four-lobed fruits begin green, then ripen to yellow at 65 to 70 days. Orobelles are fairly large and thick walled. While they are perfect raw and freeze well, they make outstanding additions to a stir-fry or a sautéed mixed pepper combination. They can also be roasted whole, making sumptuous additions to just about any course. Roast, then core, peel, and seed the peppers, leaving them as whole as possible. Serve them on a platter with steamed portobello mushrooms, extra-virgin olive oil, salt, and fresh oregano or opal basil. The plants provide plenty of peppers and resist the tobacco mosaic and potato V viruses.

Pepperoncini (C. annuum)

These sweet, mild yet tangy peppers are excellent candidates for antipasto and sweet or hot pickling mixes. The peppers grow to about 4 in. with a slightly puffy yet wrinkled look.

Sweet pickle

Vidi

These peppers are also fun to grow because the plants become loaded with fruits that ripen from light green to red. The plants almost seem to explode from buds to a profusion of peppers overnight, but in fact they yield after 65 days.

Sweet pickle (C. annuum)
Many ornamental peppers grow in Thailand or Indonesia. They provide a rainbow of beautiful colors, but as one of my colleagues attests, "they're hot enough to blow your head off!" However, this capsicum variety is different; it is ornamental and edible at the same time. It is not hot but in fact sweet and perfect for pickling.

The dark green foliage is dense on a bushy yet compact plant that grows to about 15 in. in height and yields mature fruit in 65 to 70 days. The 2-in. conical pods display bright hues of yellow, purple, orange, and red. Whether used whole and fresh in salads or pickled as a condiment, these peppers offer dense, crisp flesh, full of sweetness but no heat.

Sweet pickle peppers were developed during the 1980s in the United States. Proper cultivation of this variety yields plenty of peppers—so many that you can "pick a peck."

Vidi (C. annuum)
Vidi are known by many as the European bell. Unlike their American cousins, they are not blocky. In fact, they often grow to be longer than they are wide. These peppers are sweet and crunchy, with a yield beginning after about 65 days. The fruits ripen from a deep emerald green to a dark, rich red.

The plants are compact, erect, and bushy and produce reliably all season. The 6-in. to 7-in. elongated fruits have thick walls that are crisp when eaten raw and meaty and succulent when eaten broiled or grilled. They freeze well and retain their body when baked, sautéed, or stir-fried.

Yankee bell (C. annuum)

These open-pollinated, non-hybrid bells were originally bred for growers in northern areas. They bear green fruits that ripen to red. Plants begin to yield after 60 to 65 days and produce a consistent quantity of medium-sized, blocky peppers with smooth, thick walls. Yankee bells are good to eat raw and become pliable fairly quickly under heat.

CHILE PEPPERS

The history as well as the lore about the chile illustrate just how influential a fruit or spice can be. The chile has been lauded by explorers such as Christopher Columbus, used by the Incas to wean their babies, and stirred into the cold chocolate drink that Montezuma loved so well. Today, after centuries of study, the diverse and ancient chile yields the same benefits discovered by our forebears.

A cache of nomenclature abounds for many varieties: the jalapeño is actually a chipotle when smoked and peeled; the ancho mulato is also called the poblano when fresh and the ancho when dried; New Mexico chiles are also Big Jims, Anaheims, and a number of other cultivars that vary in flavor and heat.

While understanding chile nomenclature may seem a bit confusing, growing chiles and determining their best culinary use simply require curiosity, patience, and clement growing conditions. Above all, their ability to cross-pollinate must be respected, as their heat may travel to sweeter peppers in the same vicinity.

Ají yellow (C. baccatum)

The ají yellow is a South American pepper that could have been used in Peru as early as 2500 B.C. Its nomenclature not only refers to the specific pod, but ají is also the South American general reference to chiles. This ají is a bright green pod that can turn to orange, yellow, or brown when mature. The plants grow 4 ft. to 6 ft. in height and yield peppers

Yankee bell

Ají yellow

Anaheim

4 in. to 6 in. long. While the plants can take more than 120 days to reach maturity, they each yield more than 40 hot and sometimes fiery pods. This chile dries well and also makes for a lively addition to sauces, side dishes, and salsa.

Anaheim (C. annuum)

These California chiles are mild and meaty, adding great flavor and a little heat to other foods, especially vegetables. These long, tapered peppers add dimension to dairy products, eggs, traditional dishes such as rellenos and enchiladas, and a variety of cooked sauces.

These peppers are relatively easy to grow, with plants yielding fruit after 65 to 75 days. The chiles are 6 in. to 7 in. long and 1 in. to 2 in. wide at the top, gently tapering to the tip. The fruit begins as a bright, almost waxy green and ripens to a dark, soft red. Given the heat of some of their cousins, Anaheims make a good introduction to growing and eating chiles. They're far better than starting with the mighty little habanero!

Ancho/poblano (C. annuum)

Anchos/poblanos are short, wide chiles. When these peppers are on the plant or just harvested, they are known as poblanos or mulatos; when dried they are called anchos. These terms are often used interchangeably, causing much confusion. Poblanos begin dark green, then turn a deep red when fully matured. When dried, they are a dark red that is almost brown. Used either fresh or dried, these peppers add medium heat and impact to salsas, chile blends, soups, and main dishes.

Ancho/poblano

Caliente

Cascabel

Reaching 24 in. to 25 in. high, the compact plants grow pendant, with pods 4 in. to 6 in. in length. Plants begin to yield fruits after 50 to 55 days and consistently produce until the first frost.

Caliente (C. annuum)

These peppers begin green and mature to varying hues of flame red. The 6-in.-long pods are fairly uniform in width from their tops to their tapered ends. These thin-walled peppers have medium heat and dry easily. They're also good ornamental peppers for making attractive ropes and ristras (see pp. 46-48). You can string and dry calientes and leave them hanging until ready for grinding. The ground chile makes a good seasoning for salsas, sauces, fish, poultry, or meat. The plants begin to yield fruits after 65 days and bear abundantly until the first frost.

Cascabel (C. annuum)

These pungent chiles are named from the way the pods sound once dry. As the peppers dry, their veins fail to hold onto the seeds, allowing the seeds to fall freely within the pepper walls. The cascabel, which means "jingle bells" in Spanish, sounds like a rattle.

These peppers closely resemble the cherry pepper when maturing, but they change to a deep, reddish-brown color when dried. Cascabels are frequently used fresh in a variety of dishes such as enchiladas, but the dried chiles add an unmistakable scent and flavor. The pendant fruit matures in approximately 70 days, and plants offer a high yield when harvested frequently.

Cayenne (C. annuum)

Like dozens of other varieties, these chiles begin green and mature to a rich, bright red. Packing a kick that's felt, cayennes are a favorite flavoring for Cajun foods such as gumbos and for Asian stir-fry dishes.

These plants yield pods 6 in. to 9 in. long and about 1 in. wide. Cayenne plants are tall, bushy, and prolific, producing 35 to 50 pods.

Cherry (C. annuum)

Cherry peppers (both sweet and hot varieties) received their name because their pods look like large, red cherries. Varying from mild

Cayenne

to pungent, cherries make excellent pickling peppers. Milder cherry peppers are also good in stews and casseroles.

These plants grow well in kitchen gardens, producing round fruits about 1 in. in diameter that ripen to deep orange and red. Each plant can yield 15 to 20 pods, depending on climate and soil conditions.

Habanero (C. chinense)

Everything about the look of the habanero encourages the viewer to appreciate its heat. It is the hottest of peppers, according to many. Even the

Cherry

Habanero

Jalapeño

small, bushy plants bearing dark green, slightly heart-shaped leaves look as though they could kill any living thing within a close proximity. The small, orange pods are best dried and used in stir-fry dishes. I have added a single habanero to an entire quart of vegetables and herbs for pickling. A little does, indeed, go a very long way.

The plants typically grow to 1 ft. to 4 ft. high, depending on growing conditions. However, habanero *trees* have been known to reach 8 ft. in the tropics. Growing

to 1 in. to 2 in. long and 1 in. to 2 in. wide, habanero pods can be pointed at the end or rounded like a bonnet. They grow pendant and ripen from green to a bright, hot orange.

Jalapeño (C. annuum)

These very hot chiles are green until they fully mature to a dark red. Jalapeños offer heat to fresh table sauces, cooked salsas, and other traditional dishes that call for a blend of peppers. They are also good pickling peppers and make a flavorful

albeit heated condiment when blended with vinegar, basil, and garlic.

Jalapeños are 3 in. to 3½ in. long and ½ in. to ¾ in. across, tapering to a small, rounded point. Plants usually grow to 2 ft. high, bearing conical pods of 25 to 35 per plant.

New Mexico Joe Parker (C. annuum)

These are among many New Mexico chiles that offer high yield of meaty, fairly thick-walled pods. They are voluminous with a tangy flavor

New Mexico Joe Parker

Mirasol

without being too hot, and they adapt to just about any recipe calling for the zest and heat of chiles. Beginning in August of every year, farmer's markets are redolent with Joe Parkers roasting in their cages. These peppers, with their meatiness, can offer quarts of chile or enchilada sauce from just one bushel. Once roasted and allowed to cool, they are easy to peel and have a flavor that may be addictive. They make a zesty batch of fajita filling and an unforgettable dish of rellenos.

Growing to 2 ft. to 2½ ft. high, the plants yield pods that are 6 in. to 7 in. long and taper to a rounded point. The pods are somewhat flatter than conical hotter chiles such as jalapeños.

Mirasol (C. annuum)

Mirasol in Spanish means "to look at the sun." Mirasol chiles received their name because the pods grow upward, reaching for the sky. These bright red peppers, which start as green, mature in approximately 80 days. The fruit carries medium

heat with a distinctive hint of strawberry. Mirasols include several varieties that have been cultivated and harvested in Mexico for years, but they have recently found their way to the United States.

Pasilla (C. annuum)

Meaning "raisin" in Spanish, pasilla is the perfect name for these Mexican chiles that when dried bear the color, wrinkles, and aroma of raisins. The elongated fruits add a delicious flavor to recipes, whether used fresh

Fresh pasilla

Piquin

or dried. Plants usually grow 2 ft. to 3 ft. tall and bear hearty fruits that mature in 75 to 80 days. Pasilla is the name for the dried chilaca.

Piquin (C. annuum)

Also spelled pequin, these chiles refer to *pequeño*, which in Spanish means small. Piquin plants yield ½-in.- to 1-in.-long, bullet-shaped fruits after about 90 days. They start green and mature to red. Although these chiles have been domesticated, they also grow wild in the southwestern United States, northern Mexico, and the Andes of South America. Some chile experts believe that the domesticated and wild varieties are collected and given the broad nomenclature of piquin, so it is impossible to tell which is which. Piquins add a kick to a variety of salsa and table sauces when used green. When dried and crushed, they are nearly indispensable for soups, beans, or stews.

Serrano (C. annuum)

Serranos grow prolifically on compact, leafy plants that grow from 3 ft. to 5 ft. high, depending on conditions. The 2-in. to 4-in. pods grow pendant as well as erect, maturing after 65 to 70 days. These peppers vary in hotness yet all remain high on the heat scale. The deep

Serrano

ABOUT CHILES

From Jean Andrews, author of Peppers: "Perhaps native-born North Americans are handicapped by a late start when it comes to eating peppers, but some of us are making up for lost time. I admit that I am addicted to these zesty little fruits, and I have instructed the mockingbirds that feast on the peppers in my Texas garden to deposit seeds on my grave so that I will never run out."

Super cayenne

Tabasco

green pods ripen to red, orange, brown, or yellow. Fresh diced serranos can be added to salsas and table sauces, creating an enticing flavor combination with lime, cilantro, and a bit of coarse salt.

Super cayenne (C. annuum)

Growing 24 in. to 30 in. tall, super cayenne plants prolifically offer disease-resistant fruits after 70 to 75 days. These very hot hybrid chiles grow 4 in. to

6 in. in length and mature from green to red. The pods are best dried and used as a seasoning for pickled vegetable and cucumber mixes. The dried cayenne can be stored whole, then crushed for immediate use.

Tabasco (C. frutenscens)

Tabasco plants yield prolifically after approximately 90 days, with each plant offering hundreds of pods. The plants grow 2 ft. to 3 ft. tall, with pods borne erect. The fruits reach a length of

nearly 1⅝ in. and mature from yellow to orange to red. These peppers are, of course, the basis for the most famous hot sauce in the world. When dried and crushed, they also lend a fiery, smoky, and slightly addictive flavor to a variety of recipes calling for hot spiciness. They are especially good in Creole cuisine. Fresh tabasco pepper pulp can be mashed and added to other spices such as bay leaves, tarragon, and garlic when boiling crawfish and shrimp.

HARVESTING AND STORING

Whether harvested from your home garden or purchased as fresh produce from your local farm, peppers lose nutrients and flavor quickly once they are picked. Select your produce, handle it carefully, and process as immediately as possible for freshness and flavor retention. There are a variety of methods for storing peppers, including canning, drying, and freezing.

SELECTING PRODUCE

If you are harvesting from your garden, select peppers that have reached full size and have ripened to maturity. The more you harvest, the greater the pepper yield. Always cut rather than pull peppers from the branch or vine. The plant fiber is coarse and unyielding, so it's likely that if you pull you will ruin the pepper before getting it free of its plant.

When harvesting at home or buying from the local farm, look for peppers that have shiny, almost translucent skins covering firm pods that feel full and tight. Sweet peppers, such as bells, pimientos, and cherries, adhere to their stems through all stages of growth. However, the best chiles are those that seem to jiggle a little from their stems. If the chiles want to come away from their stems easily, they are at peak flavor and ready to use. A stem that seems a bit unyielding as you try to turn the chile means the chile still needs a little time to reach maturity.

Commercial growers select and pick produce at a slightly

Look for peppers that are bright and glossy with color. The skin should have an almost waxy translucence, and the flesh should be firm and free of spots, dents, and wrinkles.

immature state because of the time span between harvest, sale, and use. Still, peppers you buy at the market should be firm and free from bruises, spots, nicks, dents, and irregularities. Always try to find out when fruit was picked. I prefer to buy peppers no more than three days after they were picked.

HANDLING PEPPERS

Peppers, like a lot of other produce, should be handled carefully. Sweet peppers, including ethnic varieties, can be handled directly with your bare hands. However, use gloves when working with any chile hotter than mild. This includes anything with a heat rating higher than 3 (see the chart below).

Chiles contain capsaicin, an odorless chemical compound that can offer explosive heat,

---

PEPPER HEAT

Wilbur L. Scoville developed the first organoleptic test for measuring the heat of chiles in 1912. At the time, humans tasted chiles to determine their heat value, producing subjective and somewhat contradictory heat scales. Today, high-pressure chromotography measures capsaicin in Scoville units, which have become an industry standard for classifying chiles according to heat. Since environment can dramatically affect the strength of capsaicin, the heat factor can vary in peppers grown from genetically identical seeds. Here are a few of the better-known peppers along with their positions on the heat scale.

Heat rating	Scoville units	Pepper variety
10	100,000-300,000	habanero, Bahamian, tepin
9	50,000-99,999	Thai, chiltepin (wild piquin), hot banana
8	30,000-49,999	tabasco, rocotto, piquin, cayenne, ají
7	15,000-29,999	Arbol, hot cherry, serrano
6	5,000-14,999	Fresno, Santa Fe, jalapeño
5	2,500-4,999	mirasol, caliente
4	1,500-2,499	cascabel, corno di toro
3	1,000-1,499	Española, poblano, chilaca (pasilla)
2	500-999	Anaheim, New Mexico Big Jim and Joe Parker
1	100-499	Mexi bell, sweet cherry
0	0-99	pimiento, bell, Hungarian sweet wax

Because the chemical capsaicin can severely burn your skin, wear gloves when handling hot peppers of any kind. Don't remove the gloves until you've finished with the peppers, discarded the hot veins and seeds, and cleaned up the kitchen.

The seeds and veins are the hottest parts of the chile. You can remove and dry the seeds for future cultivation or culinary use, but be sure to place them in a marked container.

depending on the chile variety, growing conditions, and the age of the fruit. While immature chiles tend to be universally harmless, mature capsicums can seriously burn skin and hands that come into contact with the compound. Chile eaters love the sensation of warmth that fills the mouth, but that same warmth can add a lingering sting to eyes, ears, and sensitive skin. You have a long time to wait if your eye is in pain, so wear gloves. If you do have an accident, cool water will provide temporary relief without really healing the injury. Like many organic compounds, capsaicin does dissolve in alcohol, though. So try using

a rinse of rubbing alcohol on the afflicted skin areas.

STORING PEPPERS

Cooks and kitchen gardeners have a variety of options for preserving the flavor and freshness of the harvest.

Once you get your peppers home, wash them in cold water and allow them to air dry or pat them gently with a lint-free towel. If you don't plan to use the peppers immediately, place them in air-tight plastic bags and

Some basic items necessary for canning include a boiling-water-bath canner, sterile jars, lids, rims, funnels, and clamps for retrieving hot jars.

refrigerate. They can stay crisp and full of flavor for a day or two as you prepare to process. They can, in certain climates, remain firm and fresh in a cool, fairly dry basement for two to three weeks.

Since peppers are a low-acid vegetable and spice, some

processing methods yield better results than others. The greatest loss of vitamins and minerals often results from how food is prepared. Vitamin B_1, riboflavin, and niacin dissolve quickly in cooking water, since these are water-soluble vitamins. Vitamins A and C, of which peppers have an exceptional amount, break down readily when exposed to any method that requires heat.

Here are some of the advantages and disadvantages of certain processing methods and how they affect sweet and hot varieties.

Canning and preserving
Low-acid foods such as peppers don't retain flavor or color well when canned alone. It's best to use the peppers in the preparation of salsas, sauces, condiments, and special blends such as chutneys. These foods rely on a combination of flavors and usually require ingredients such as vinegar, salt, and sugar that arrest the enzyme activity that decomposes harvested fruits and vegetables. Peppers can be hot packed or cold packed. Regardless of the variety or the storing process, certain simple yet critical rules

should be followed to ensure successful results. Most canning guides and state agricultural extension services provide information specific to various regions of the country.

Before you begin canning, gather the necessary items. These include a boiling-water-bath canner or pressure canner, jars, lids, rims, funnels, clamps, racks, hot pads, and long-handled dippers and spoons.

Here are some canning tips regardless of your geographic region.

- Make sure all utensils and jars are sterile and hot for use.

- Check jar rims for cracks and lids for possible inconsistencies in the rubber seal. Such irregularities can prevent the jar from pressure sealing to an air-tight state. If this happens, food will spoil within 24 hours.

- Wipe the rims of the jars with a clean, damp cloth to pick up any stray particles of food. Any little bit that sits on the seal or rim will more than likely prevent the jar from achieving a vacuum state. Again, the result will be spoiled food.

- If you're using a pressure canner, check the dial gauge, which registers the pounds of steam pressure being produced, for accuracy each year before you begin to can. Gauges can be checked at most county extension agencies. If the gauge reads more than one pound on the high side of 5, 10, or 15 pounds of pressure, you run the risk of under-processing. If your gauge reads low, you may process longer than needed. In either case, replace the gauge. Since gauges are delicate mechanisms, follow the package instructions for their care and use.

- Use pint or half-pint jars only. Because peppers tend to spoil or lose their texture and flavor easily, you don't want to use large jars that will be frequently opened, letting in oxygen. Since peppers will probably be pickled or used as a condiment, you don't want the burden of storing something for several weeks in your

While all utensils must be sterile, the caps play a critical role. The rubber gasket should be clean, dry, and free of nicks or irregularities that could interfere with the formation of a seal.

refrigerator. Celebrating the harvest doesn't mean making more food than you can realistically consume.

- Look for spoilage in canned foods. If you see a bulge in the lid, open the jar. If the food has a sour, acid taste or odor or if mold is visible, food spoilage is occurring that can, as in the case of botulism, be poisonous.

Hot packing
This method of precooking before canning provides important benefits for peppers and other low-acid foods with little protection against harmful bacteria. Packing hot food into hot jars that are then processed at 240°F ensures the death of microorganisms that thrive in alkaline environments.

When packing peppers in oil or in another liquid, heat the liquid or sauce until bubbling, then pour into hot jars and process. If you are using a boiling-water bath, hot food may require less processing time than raw-packed food. If you are using a pressure canner, the processing time remains the same for hot or raw ingredients. Food acidity and

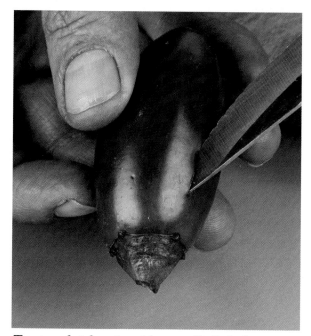

Smaller peppers like the jalapeño make delicious pickles. Trim the stems before placing the pods in the jar to decrease the likelihood of bruising, since bruised fruit won't keep long in the pantry.

Treat each jalapeño with a small slit before packing into the jar, so the vinegar, herbs, and spices will permeate each pepper.

altitude determine the recommended method of processing. Be sure to check a reliable canning guide before you begin.

Cold packing

Since peppers lose their vitamins and color readily under heat, using the cold-packing method for pickled peppers is recommended. Peppers make great pickled condiments (see the photos above and on the facing page for the pickling sequence).

Some cooks will use equal parts of water, cider vinegar, and spice for pickling. However, I prefer using 100 percent distilled white vinegar combined with herbs and spices or salt. You may or may not want to include salt when heating the liquid. I sometimes place the salt in the bottom of the jar before adding the peppers and brine.

In any case, clip the stems of flawless, raw peppers and pack the peppers into hot jars gently, making sure that the fruit remains free from bruises. Cover with the boiling liquid. Insert a plastic knife, chopstick, or other pointed instrument down the side of the jar to push unwanted air bubbles to the top. With less oxygen, the jars will seal tighter. Process in a boiling-water bath for 15 to 20 minutes depending on the altitude. If you process too long, the peppers will lose their color and crunch. They will probably taste okay but won't have zing, which is the purpose of the process.

Whether you are hot packing or cold packing, allow the jars to stand in a draft-free area

After placing the peppers in the jar, insert raw garlic cloves into any crevices. Do the same with opal basil or any other herb you use.

Pour the boiling vinegar into the packed jars, leaving ¼-in. headspace. The peppers should be at least ½ in. below the surface of the solution.

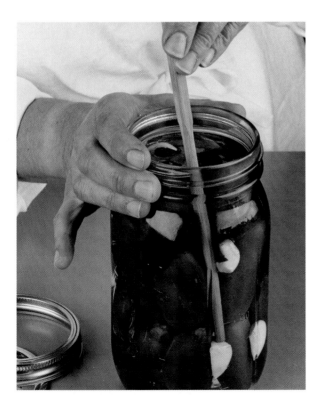

Use a chopstick or knife to force air bubbles to the top of the jar. The air bubbles should rise to the top before, not during, the canning process, thus encouraging a complete seal.

To dry a pepper whole, cut off the stem and cap and slit the pod lengthwise from top to bottom.

Use your hands or a knife to remove the seeds and veins from the pepper. It can now be dried.

until the lids have popped, then transfer them to a dry, cool pantry. Most preserved foods should sit for about two weeks before serving.

Drying

It's true that peppers adapt well to canning or freezing, but peppers, especially chiles, retain their flavor and heat best when dried. Since peppers are a spice, a condiment, and a vegetable, they are adaptable to a wide variety of uses when dried. Dried ground chile is easy to store in jars or freezer bags. You can keep it in a cool, dark pantry or the refrigerator for up to a year. Dried whole or ground chile keeps very well for extended periods of time in the freezer.

Dried peppers require little space, since they can be ground and stored in jars or stored in pieces at about one-third of their original bulk. Sweet and hot peppers can be left whole, cut into strips, or diced for drying. Drying extracts water, which contains organisms, to greatly reduce bacterial growth. Drying ensures against bacterial growth far more than canning does. While hotter, drier climates produce hotter peppers, dehydration removes even more water from the pod, thus intensifying flavor and color.

Dried peppers' concentrated flavor is enhanced when the peppers are reconstituted. Both hot and sweet peppers can be reconstituted by soaking them in hot water for 15 to 20 minutes. When chiles are then fried in a little oil or lightly roasted, they puff up to their original size very quickly.

While processing tends to break down their nutrients, peppers are still good for

Open a dried chile pod by removing the stem and top first. Pour out the loose seeds, then break the pepper open from top to bottom for easier removal of additional seeds that may still be attached.

Some of the more popular dried chiles include (clockwise from top right) the tabasco, cascabel, pequin, New Mexico, and pasilla. The mirasol is shown at center.

you—they just don't pack the same vitamin punch as when eaten raw and fresh. Since peppers are more susceptible to decay than high-acid fruits, drying is highly recommended. It's also the oldest and simplest method for preserving and storing food for future use.

The following methods provide drying options for various cultivars and areas of the country.

Sun drying

This method of drying peppers outdoors works well for people who live in hot, dry climates with an average-to-long growing season. Since this process requires two to three consecutively sunny days, it's not recommended for northern regions or climates high in humidity. However, if you live in a place that makes sun drying easy, you can

make your own frames and dehydrate your peppers during the day, remembering to bring them indoors at night.

To construct a frame, I prefer to use wood that is 2 in. to 3 in. wide and no more than 1 in. thick. Frames that are 16-in. to 18-in. squares or 16-in. by 18-in. rectangles are reasonable sizes for lifting once they contain food. After nailing the wood together, nail cheesecloth to the bottom. Place the peppers on the cheesecloth, then cover with another layer of cheesecloth to protect the peppers from insects.

The screen method works well for sweet peppers, and they will shrivel, darken, and look leathery when done. Air drying also works well for medium- and thin-fleshed chiles such as jalapeños, mirasols, and cayennes. When drying peppers, rinse them and dry them with a towel. If desired, slit the sides of the peppers to accelerate drying. Place the peppers on the cheesecloth frames and set out to dry, turning them occasionally to allow the sun to penetrate the complete pepper. If you begin sun drying and the weather changes, you can finish drying the food on a baking sheet in the oven at 150°F to 200°F. Check the peppers every hour.

Although chiles can be screen dried, they dry more easily when the entire plants are hung or when the peppers are strung into ristras (see the following section). Drying the whole plant or stringing a ristra isn't recommended for moister, cooler climates. If you live in a hot, dry climate, you can dry the plants by simply ceasing to water them once they stop producing. Leave the plants in the ground, then pull them up before the first frost.

Once peppers are completely dried, they can be stored in clean, air-tight jars or immediately ground into powders or spice blends for future use. Drying allows the cook to create combinations for chile blends, paprika, and curry.

To grind hot peppers, you may or may not remove the seeds, depending on the heat of the pepper and your desires. The peppers can be ground in a spice processor or coffee grinder until they reach the desired consistency. For a coarser powder, you can use a mortar and pestle. If using a coffer grinder, clean it free from hot pepper flakes by processing with rice or coarse sea salt. Otherwise, your morning coffee will offer a few eye-openers you hadn't counted on!

Ristras
Since I live in Colorado, driving to Sante Fe, Taos, or Albuquerque during late summer provides one of the most colorful and palate-pleasing events of the harvest. Ristras, handstrung ropes of chiles, blanket the New Mexico landscape in rich, warm, red hues. Various sizes of chiles hang from roofs, porches, barns, and verandas, all reflecting a celebration and ceremony of thanks to the earth that provides food for its inhabitants.

Use a coffee grinder on dried paprika to attain the fine red powder that marries redolence and a unique flavor with food.

To clean your coffee grinder, cover the bottom of the coffee tub with 1 tablespoon coarse sea salt and turn on the grinder. The salt will push even the smallest pepper flake out from under the gears.

Tradition has it that the ristra was a symbol of the harvest and of bounty. The weary traveler could count on a little rest and at least a bit of something to eat from houses where ristras hung. The lack of ristras at a home meant that the harvest may have been poor or that there simply wasn't enough food to share.

Various New Mexico chiles dry well in a ristra, but this method is also good for pequins, cascabels, and hot wax peppers. Always use mature, red, freshly picked chile pods. Don't attempt to string green pods with the hope that they'll turn red. A ristra 3 ft. long requires about three-quarters of a bushel of peppers, depending on their sizes. Smaller chiles may use up a whole bushel.

To make a ristra, tie three chiles together with a string (see illustrations on p. 48). Continue to tie clusters until you have 10 to 15 clusters on each of two strings. Then braid them together onto a central string. I have also strung peppers one by one by using a needle and thread, pushing the needle through the stem of the chile. Just remember not to gather the peppers in a clump, so that they get plenty of air. Ristras dry well outdoors in hot, dry climates. Otherwise, hang ristras indoors in a dry, well-ventilated place. Peppers can remain on their ristras until ready for use.

Food dehydrators
Peppers yield intense flavor and retain more of their color when dried in a food dehydrator. A dehydrator has both the heat and the air circulation to effectively dry thick, fleshy chiles. Wash, dry, and cut the chiles in halves, slices, or smaller pieces. Then follow the instructions that came with your unit.

Ovens
If you don't own a dehydrator, try using your oven. Preheat the oven to 200°F to 225°F. Put the chiles in a shallow baking pan or on a baking sheet. Turn them every 30 minutes for about eight hours, or until they are dry but not too toasty. Using an oven doesn't produce dried chiles as reliably as the sun or dehydrator, so be careful of the amount of

MAKING A RISTRA

1. Make a cluster of three peppers, using a piece of string to tie them together.

2. Wrap the string around the stems two times, then loop it under, then upward between two of the pods. Tighten the string to secure the stems.

3. Making a half hitch with the string, place it over the stems and pull tight again. This ensures that the clusters will remain intact as you make the ristra. Continue to cluster and tie pods until you have 10 to 15 clusters on each of two strings.

4. The chile clusters are ready for braiding to a longer length of twine. Suspend the twine from the top of a door, horizontal rod, or rafter. Make a loop at the bottom of the twine. Tie the two strings of clusters at the loop, and braid the clusters with the twine. As you braid, keep the center twine pushed down beneath the clusters, making the clusters protrude from the center.

5. The finished ristra.

humidity in the air as well as the heat of your oven. Chiles need dry heat combined with circulating air. Since your oven provides heat but no air circulation, in a humid area, pods will turn dark and some may even spoil before they dry. However, this method is worth a try with just a few chiles. Then you'll know what works best for your climate.

Freezing

Most varieties of sweet peppers and chile peppers can be frozen. The fruits of sweet peppers such as bells and bananas should contain firm, bright flesh that is free from bruises, nicks, and other irregularities that can affect preservation.

Bell peppers

Sweet peppers should be washed whole and drained or patted dry with a lint-free towel before they are cut or chopped. If you plan to freeze pepper strips, halves, or even whole peppers, remove the stems, seeds, and veins. You will probably need to rinse the cut peppers a second time to thoroughly remove seeds or veins. Allow the bells to dry for about an hour before freezing to avoid

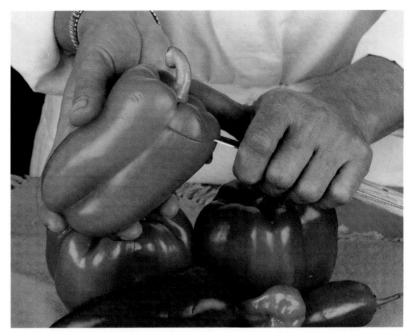

To prepare a bell pepper for freezing, remove the stem and cap with a serrated knife. Discard the stem, but add the cap to the rest of the pepper to be frozen.

Carefully remove the pepper's veins and seeds with a knife. The pepper can be halved, as shown here, left whole, or sliced into strips for freezing.

Resealable freezer bags allow plenty of flexibility for strips or large pieces of peppers, but whole peppers should be stored in plastic containers.

the formation of frost on the skin and flesh.

The peppers are now ready for placement in resealable freezer bags or plastic containers. Fill the bags one-half to two-thirds full, gently pressing the sides of the bag together until all air is removed. Pepper halves and strips make good candidates for the freezer because they don't occupy much room.

Various sources indicate that blanching hot peppers before freezing is not needed, but that blanching sweet peppers is optional. I prefer to freeze sweet peppers in their raw state. They taste better and retain their shape better when cooked. Blanching peppers can add an unwanted pungency to your freezer as well as to some of the other foods in it, despite your best efforts to make sure everything is tightly sealed. Freezing raw peppers also allows them to retain most of their nutritional value, while blanching causes a significant reduction in vitamins C, E, and B_6.

Chiles

Because chiles' skin is densely tough and fibrous, chiles should be roasted and can be peeled before freezing. After removing the skins, seeds, and stems, chop or slice the chiles and place them in resealable freezer bags. When ready for use, the chiles should be added to your recipes in a partially frozen state.

Here are some tips and techniques for freezing bell or chile peppers:

• Work with the most sanitary conditions, including clean kitchen counters, clean food, clean storage containers or bags, and clean hands.

• Use smaller bags for easier storage; you may end up putting more units in the freezer, but each individual unit doesn't take up much room. Also, larger bags would be opened more often, each time allowing new oxygen to enter that can eventually change the texture and flavor of the food.

• Plastic or cardboard containers can also be used to freeze peppers.

• Label containers with an indelible marker. Ballpoint ink, crayons, or pencil will fade.

• Be sure your freezer reads 0°F or colder, as oxidation begins to occur in temperatures above that. At 10°F to 15°F, foods will oxidize at a steady rate, resulting in a loss of nutrients and usability.

• Neither bell nor chile peppers need to defrost completely before use. They can be added to whatever you are cooking or can be stuffed once they are soft enough to move.

COOKING AND BAKING

Sweet peppers as well as chiles contain a volume of flavor and nutrients that contribute to the overall freshness and taste of foods. Like most produce, peppers are at their nutritional best when used fresh. Yet peppers can render a more intense flavor when dried, since the water contained in the pods evaporates, thus allowing chemical compounds to concentrate.

To preserve the freshness of most peppers, use them raw. Some varieties, such as the pasilla, tabasco, cascabel, or mirasol, add dimension to sauces and salsas when freshly ground. However, their resonance and aroma are unmistakable when they are dried and crushed for soups, stews, beans, and other dishes.

You can also sauté fresh peppers slightly, adding them to a dish as its last ingredient. Otherwise, the longer a pepper cooks, the more its flavors carry into other ingredients. Various bell peppers and chiles are delicious roasted or stuffed and baked. While peppers retain more nutrients when raw, their flavor appeal can heighten when roasted and baked. For instance, the poblano, at least to me, displays its very best flavor when roasted and baked for rellenos.

FOOD COMBINATIONS

Peppers make interesting flavor combinations with a variety of foods. Here are some of my favorite combinations.

Mixing bells of all colors— green, yellow, orange, red, and purple—offers a a blend of sweetness and body. Serve them together as a side dish, or add them to rice or pasta or to other vegetables such as tomatoes. I have used raw and slightly cooked variations with success. Peppers also blend well with herbs and other spices, such as green and purple basil, garlic, oregano, chives, tarragon, cloves, fennel, and cumin. Bells and other sweet peppers provide a good flavor contrast when blended with citrus such as tangerines, oranges, lemons, limes, or grapefruits. Chiles offer wonderful flavor combinations when mixed with almost any tropical fruit, such as papayas, mangos, kiwis, or bananas graced with a dash of lime and brown sugar.

Both sweet and hot varieties blend well with onions, garlic, tomatoes, mushrooms, and corn. Peppers provide balance and contrast to pasta, rice, beans, cheese, eggs, meats, fish, and poultry. The key lies in contrasts: Mixing pungent and savory foods with milder or sweeter food and herbs creates a contrast and balance that appeals to the taste buds.

ROASTING

There's nothing quite like the scent of chiles roasting in the open air or bell peppers sizzling on the grill. Roasting adds flavor and romance to sweet and hot varieties and fills the air with a lingering smoky redolence.

Sweet peppers

Sweet peppers are delicious roasted and easy enough to prepare about one hour before a meal. To roast sweet peppers under the broiler, over a gas burner, or on the grill, place the peppers whole on a baking sheet or in a roasting pan. Cook the peppers about 6 in. from the heat source, turning them every 3 to 5 minutes. When the peppers are blistered and browned on all sides, remove them from the heat.

The peppers can be hot packed in pint jars along with herbs, olive oil, or their own juice. I like to place the peppers along with garlic in hot jars, then cover the peppers with hot olive oil, seal, and process. I have also roasted peppers in a 425°F to 450°F oven in a deep pan that contains enough white wine vinegar to cover the bottom by ¼ in. Once the peppers are sufficiently blistered, I remove them from the pan and add the pan juices to equal amounts of water and wine vinegar for processing. The quantity of liquid required can be found in your favorite canning guide. If you have the equivalent of six pints of peppers, then find the liquid required for that quantity.

Whether roasting sweet peppers for immediate use or for canning, wait until the peppers are cool enough to handle to begin peeling them. It is preferable to peel from the top down, but some peppers have a mind of their own. I can remember peeling from bottom to top on more than one occasion. The key lies in finding a spot on the pepper that will allow you to remove a large sheaf of skin

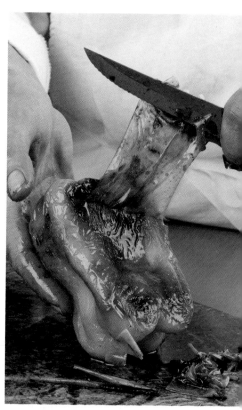

To peel a roasted sweet pepper, hold the pepper near its crown and stem. Using a sharp serrated knife, remove the skin from the base of the fruit, pulling it up toward the top. Then carefully cut out the stem and seed membrane.

at once, as opposed to peeling the skin off in little bits. While some cooks recommend peeling peppers under cold water, it may not always be necessary. Much depends upon the thickness of the pepper's flesh and how sturdy it is for handling. For instance, the skin of a thick-walled yellow bell comes off easily without the use of water. But water is helpful in peeling thinner-fleshed peppers that would otherwise tear easily when handled.

In addition, not all roasted sweet peppers need to be peeled. Varieties of cubanelles, Italian sweets (sometimes called frying peppers), some pimientos, and sweet gypsy peppers don't really require it. Leaving the skin on, as well as not rinsing peppers under cold water, allows the pepper to retain volume and flavor. Get acquainted with different pepper varieties and experiment with various techniques and flavors in order to decide upon your preferences.

Chiles

While roasting chiles offers no more of a challenge than roasting sweet peppers, peeling chiles remains a different matter. Since their skins are fibrous and rather unpalatable, most larger chiles, such as Anaheims, poblanos, and New Mexico varieties, require roasting for any type of use. Whether you are fortunate enough to

purchase chiles that are already roasted or you blister them yourself, place them while they're still hot in a paper or plastic bag and close the top of the bag tightly with a twist tie or a knot. You can also use a resealable bag if you have a very small quantity of peppers. This process causes condensation, and as the peppers cool, both the flesh and the skin contract and the two pull away from each other.

I used paper bags for years but became a convert to doubled, large plastic bags the first time I decided to cook Mexican cuisine for 50 people. I purchased the daunting amount of about 30 pounds of roasted chiles from a local vendor. I stood and watched as he placed one large plastic bag inside another, followed by the peppers. When I said I thought you were supposed to use paper, he said he preferred plastic. "They are more air tight, and you can tie the top in a knot," he said. "You've got to make them sweat." At this point, his confident grin left no question in my mind. Once home, I found that the chiles were easier to peel and that I

was able to remove the skin consistently, even from peppers with thin walls.

Removing the skin while rinsing the pepper under cold water speeds up the process, particularly if several pounds of peppers need to be peeled. It's pretty simple to rinse and rub skin off simultaneously. However, as with roasted sweet peppers, peeling without rinsing does enhance the flavor.

Remember that unless you are working with very mild chiles, *always wear plastic gloves*. Chiles contain capsaicin, an irritating, searing chemical compound that is not soluble in water (see pp. 38-39).

Here are some tips for roasting sweet or hot peppers:

- Charring or blistering the pepper doesn't mean it needs to be totally black. The blistering should add a nice roasted flavor to the pepper, not a burnt flavor that will pervade the entire capsicum if the fruit gets too seared.

- You don't need to remove every fleck of skin when

peeling peppers, especially chiles. It's almost impossible to completely remove the peel because there are areas on the surface of the peppers that simply adhere more closely to the skin. You simply want to remove skin that detracts from the enjoyment of your food.

- If you want more flavor from the roasted pepper, don't rinse it under cool water.

- It's best to work with small batches of peppers at a time because roasting and peeling peppers is a time-consuming process. You can achieve satisfying results without dedicating a half or even a whole day of work required to peel a quantity of 10 to 15 pounds, which can be from 40 to 60 peppers, depending upon their size. The process should be enjoyable.

STUFFING PEPPERS

Sweet peppers, such as red, yellow, and orange bells, as well as cubanelles and several varieties of New Mexico chiles, make delicious meals when stuffed. The poblano, in particular,

The mild poblano is a perfect chile for stuffing. When the roasted pepper is cool enough to handle, loosen the skin at the base of the pepper and gently pull it all the way to the stem to remove.

has the size, texture, and flavor that make it a perfect pepper for stuffing (see the recipe on p. 62). While peppers can be stuffed with just about anything from cheese to vegetables to fish and meats, the flavor can change dramatically with the choice. Stuffing a chile with a simple mixture of corn, cumin, cilantro, and a blend of cheeses or cheese and sour cream creates a balanced flavor combination where the pungency of the pepper and the creamy, tangy corn-cheese blend enhance each other. But I find that stuffing a pepper with too much meat or cheese overwhelms the aroma and piquant taste that I seek when eating chiles. In

Once peeled, slit the pepper lengthwise and gently remove the seeds, veins, and, if desired, the stem with your thumb and index finger.

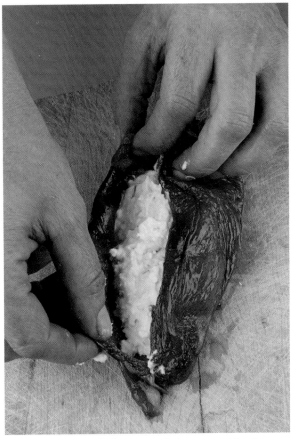

To stuff the pepper, lay it flat. Spoon 3 to 4 table-spoons of your favorite mixture onto the pepper from top to bottom, leaving about ¾ in. of space on either side of the filling.

To close the stuffed pepper, bring one side then the other over the filling. One side should flap over the other to ensure that the pepper remains closed.

addition, larger or chunkier pieces of food can impede the ease of wrapping the chile around the stuffing. However, the flavor combination chosen is entirely up to the cook.

I roast and peel the pepper, then carefully slit the pepper along its side from top to bottom and remove the seeds and veins. The stem can be removed or left attached, depending upon personal preference.

To stuff the pepper, lay it flat and gently spoon 3 to 4 tablespoons of the filling onto it. Leave about ¾ in. of space on either side of the filling, making sure that there is enough filling without making the pepper bulge or even teat. Close the pepper by bringing the sides of the chile up around the filling toward the middle, with one side overlapping the other. If the pepper doesn't close completely, remove some of the filling. Place the pepper slit side down in a baking dish. It's now ready to be an ingredient in your favorite casserole or rellenos dish or eaten as an appetizer.

RECIPES

APPETIZERS

Yellow Bell or Sweet Banana Pepper Botanas
(recipe on page 60)

Yellow Bell or Sweet Banana Pepper Botanas

*In Mexico, botana means appetizer. The combination
of flavors in this yellow pepper version offers a more mellow sweetness
than other recipes calling for a mixture of capsicum and cheese. The unique complement
of flavors blends well with a platter of chilled marinated shrimp. Add grilled
vegetables, and you have dinner for guests. (Photo on page 58.)*

HEAT SCALE: *mild*
BEST USE: *fresh*

12 sweet banana peppers, or 6
   very small yellow bell peppers
one 24-ounce container of ricotta
   cheese, thoroughly drained
2 large cloves garlic, crushed
¼ cup crumbled Gorgonzola
   cheese
1 teaspoon crushed tabasco
   chile, or 1 teaspoon red
   pepper flakes
1 tablespoon orange juice
salt, to taste
½ cup coarsely chopped toasted
   pecans, garnish

Wash and split the peppers
lengthwise. Remove all seeds and
veins. Set aside. Blend the ricotta,
garlic, Gorgonzola, tabasco chile,
and orange juice in a medium
bowl with a fork or whisk. Season
with salt.

Fill the pepper halves with the
cheese mixture and garnish with
the toasted pecans. Serve cold.

Yields 12-24 botanas

*Note: This recipe can be made up to
8 hours prior to serving.*

CROSTINI WITH ANCHOVIES, PEPPERS, AND CAPERS

*Since this anchovy mixture is blended by hand, you can choose a fork
or a mortar and pestle to achieve the desired consistency. When mixed with a fork,
the ingredients form a loose, chunky trio. To create a smoother consistency, you can gently mash the
mixture with a fork or use a mortar and pestle. However, don't use a blender or food processor because that will
combine the colors, leaving the hues of green, yellow, and chestnut indistinct. These crostini are also fun
with a little orange or lemon zest on top. Crostini, like its cousins bruschetta and fett'unta,
offer a variety of opportunities for creative light meals as well as appetizer feasts.*

HEAT SCALE: **mild**
BEST USE: **fresh**

Toasts
1 slender French baguette or
    crusty loaf of Italian bread
⅓-½ cup extra-virgin olive oil
salt and freshly ground black
    pepper, to taste

Topping
6 anchovy fillets, minced
1 yellow bell pepper, finely
    chopped
juice of 1 lemon
2 tablespoons fresh oregano, or
    1 teaspoon dried
2 tablespoons drained capers,
    rinsed
1 tablespoon extra-virgin olive oil
freshly ground white pepper,
    to taste

For the toasts, preheat the oven to 350°F.

Slice the bread in round or diagonal slices. Brush the bread on both sides with the olive oil and arrange in a single layer on a baking sheet. Season lightly with salt and pepper.

Bake on the middle rack of the oven 7-10 minutes. Turn the slices over and bake about 7 minutes longer, or until golden. Allow the toasts to cool to room temperature before use.

For the topping, mix all of the topping ingredients in a small bowl. Spoon onto the crostini and serve immediately.

Serves 6 (yields 1 cup topping)

Note: The bread toasts store well in a tin or air-tight container for 2-3 weeks.

ROASTED AND STUFFED POBLANOS

*The combination of chiles and citrus offers an enticing
zest to appetizers, main dishes, and desserts. These stuffed poblanos can
be enjoyed as a light lunch with cheeses and warmed tortillas or as the herald for dinner. Try them
with an iced tea or frosty beer to balance the slight, creamy sting that comes from the chiles, cheese,
and sour cream. You can, of course, eat these with a fork and knife,
but they're more fun to eat with your hands.*

HEAT SCALE: **medium to
  medium-hot**
BEST USE: **fresh**

6 large shrimp, steamed, shelled,
  deveined, and chopped
1 large navel orange, peeled and
  diced
¼ cup pineapple juice
2 cloves garlic, crushed
¼ teaspoon ground cloves
¼ cup sour cream
8 ounces cream cheese, softened
6-8 poblano chiles, roasted,
  peeled, and seeded
½ cup fresh lime juice
1 teaspoon salt

In a medium bowl, blend the shrimp, oranges, pineapple juice, garlic, and cloves with a fork. Add the sour cream and cream cheese, stirring gently until the mixture is smooth yet slightly chunky.

Using a tablespoon, fill the poblanos with the mixture, but do not overstuff them. Close each poblano by wrapping one side of the pepper, then the other, around the filling. Place the poblanos on a serving platter and refrigerate 10 minutes.

In a small cup, whisk the lime juice and salt. After removing the platter from the refrigerator, pour a little of the juice over each poblano and serve.

Serves 6-8

PEPPER-DRESSED ARTICHOKE HEARTS

*This appetizer can be prepared ahead of time, which makes it a good candidate
for serving a large or small group of guests. The combination of green from the lettuce,
pink from the shrimp, and golden yellow from the sauce creates a colorful yet light look for the table.
It's especially refreshing in the summer when served with grilled poultry or fish, tossed salad,
and focaccia. It also provides balance for heartier winter soups and stews.*

HEAT SCALE: *mild*
BEST USE: *fresh*

6 tablespoons extra-virgin olive oil
2 tablespoons lemon juice
1 teaspoon lemon zest
1 tablespoon white wine vinegar
3 tablespoons grated Parmesan
   cheese
2 cloves garlic, minced
1 Hungarian sweet pepper,
   roasted, peeled, seeded, and
   coarsely chopped
12 canned artichoke hearts,
   (a 14-ounce can yields 5 large
   hearts)
6 large leaves romaine lettuce,
   sliced
6 large shrimp, steamed, shelled,
   deveined, and chopped
salt and ground red pepper,
   to taste

In a small bowl, blend the oil, lemon juice, lemon zest, vinegar, and cheese with a whisk. Add the garlic and peppers. Pour the mixture into a screw-top jar and refrigerate overnight. Remove the artichokes from the can, drain, and refrigerate overnight.

Remove the artichokes and the dressing from the refrigerator 15-20 minutes before serving. Cut the artichokes into quarters.

Line a plate with the sliced romaine. Set the artichokes on the romaine, and spoon the shrimp onto each.

Shake the dressing thoroughly and pour over the artichoke hearts. Season with salt and a dash of ground red pepper. Serve immediately.

Serves 6

Note: The artichokes may also be served after marinating in the refrigerator overnight. The sauce keeps well refrigerated for up to 1 week.

GRILLED PRAWNS

*I sometimes call these the prawns of October, since I make
this dish most frequently during the fall when tomatoes and jalapeño
chiles still carry the zest of the harvest. Blend the mixture well, so that it
doesn't fall out of the shrimp until you are ready to let it fall into your
mouth. The prawns should be pink and tender, but not too firm.*

HEAT SCALE: *medium*
BEST USE: *fresh*

4 plum tomatoes, seeded and
   chopped
2 jalapeño chiles, seeded,
   deveined, and minced
2 tablespoons fresh minced
   cilantro
juice of 1 lime
3 tablespoons extra-virgin olive oil
12 jumbo or tiger shrimp, shelled,
   deveined, and butterflied

Preheat the grill to medium-hot.
Mix the tomatoes, chiles, cilantro,
lime juice, and oil in a medium
bowl. Place the shrimp on a heat-
proof pan or screen, then spoon
the mixture into and around the
shrimp. Hold the shrimp together
with a toothpick, if necessary.
Cover and grill 7-10 minutes.
Serve immediately.

Serves 6-12

CAPONATA

During the summer and early fall, batches of caponata fill the kitchen counter. I can recall a story from my mother who says that when she was a child, "everyone in the neighborhood became vegetarian in August. That's when we ate eggplant. We couldn't wait to grill it, mix it with pasta, eat it in sandwiches, and make caponata. We had a feast...."

HEAT SCALE: *mild*
BEST USE: *fresh or canned*

1 firm medium eggplant (about
   1 pound)
½ cup extra-virgin olive oil
8 ribs celery hearts, diced
2 medium onions, chopped
2 red bell peppers, seeded
   and chopped
1½ teaspoons salt
2 pounds plum tomatoes, seeded
   and chopped
2 tablespoons chopped fresh
   parsley
2 tablespoons crumbled dried
   celery leaves
8 large cloves garlic, thinly sliced
2 teaspoons fresh thyme leaves
¼ cup balsamic vinegar
1 tablespoon sugar
1 tablespoon dried oregano
1 cup black olives, pitted
1 cup drained, Cerignola green
   olives
¼ cup drained capers, rinsed
freshly ground black pepper,
   to taste

Rinse the unpeeled eggplant, chop it into ½-inch or ¾-inch cubes, and set aside.

In a large frying pan, heat ¼ cup of the oil over medium-low heat, and sauté the fresh celery until translucent. Remove the celery from the pan and set aside.

In another large, 2-inch-deep frying pan, heat the remaining oil over medium heat. Sauté the onions and peppers until translucent and slightly tender. Add the salt, tomatoes, parsley, dried celery, and garlic, and simmer 20 minutes (the vegetables should be firm). Lower the heat and add the fresh celery and thyme. Stir all of the ingredients, cook 5 minutes, remove the mixture from the heat, and set aside.

Cook the eggplant in the frying pan used for the celery over medium heat, about 5 minutes (the eggplant should remain firm). Stir in the vinegar.

Add the eggplant to the tomato mixture, along with the sugar, oregano, olives, and capers. Season with pepper. Serve at room temperature.

If canning, allow the mixture to cook over medium-high heat until bubbly. Pour into hot, sterilized jars, leaving ¼-inch headspace. Screw the lids and rings tightly on the jars, and process 20 minutes in a boiling-water bath. Remove the jars from the water and let stand in a draft-free area until the lids have popped.

Yields 4 pints

Note: This dish is good served with fresh bread and provolone or Asiago cheese.

BRIE WITH PEPPERS, MANGOS, AND TOASTED ALMONDS

*This appetizer is delicious alone or with a plate of kiwi, papaya,
strawberries, and Tuscany toast crostini as an accompaniment. The cheese,
peppers, and lime create a pleasant and tangy blend of flavors. I like to serve this appetizer
with penne and peppers along with a crisp Frascati white wine for supper. This appetizer also
works well when preparing dinner for guests, since the chile mix can be prepared
in advance and added to the brie when ready to heat and serve.*

HEAT SCALE: **medium**
BEST USE: **fresh**

1 round brie, about 5 inches
   in diameter (13-16 ounces),
   slightly chilled
1 red bell pepper, roasted,
   peeled, seeded, and chopped
2 jalapeño chiles, seeded,
   deveined, and chopped
1 mango, diced
juice of 1 lime
½ cup roasted almond pieces

Preheat the oven to 350°F.

Using a paring knife, cut a 1-inch-deep circle about 4 inches in diameter in the brie. Scoop out the circle with a fork to leave a 1-inch rim in the top of the brie. Allow the cheese to warm to room temperature.

Mix the bell peppers, chiles, mangos, and lime juice in a small bowl and set aside.

Place the brie on an ovenproof dish, and bake 10-15 minutes, or until warm and slightly soft. Remove from the oven and spoon on the pepper mixture. Cover with the roasted almonds and serve immediately.

Serves 12

*Brie with Peppers, Mangos,
and Toasted Almonds (recipe this page)*

PEPPER-OLIVE TAPENADE

*The Alphonso olive adds a little spice and bitterness to the smooth, sweet flavor
of ripe olives. It is imported from Chile and can be found in the specialty-food section
in markets or shops that carry ethnic ingredients. The Alphonso is huge and comes packed in brine.
The deep purple flesh should be firm and crisp. As with many recipes, substitutions do work. I have used
Italian Gaeta olives and French niçoise olives instead of the Alphonso. The Greek Amphissa is another
purple, brine-packed olive that is full of fruity flavor and is easy to find at the market. The olive
you choose depends upon the type of flavor you enjoy. ✍ This tapenade is delicious
when used to top halved fresh plum tomatoes or slices of fresh mozzarella.
I have even tried it tossed with cooked egg or tomato linguine.*

HEAT SCALE: *mild*
BEST USE: *fresh*

1 purple bell pepper, seeded
   and coarsley chopped
1 cup ripe olives, drained
3 Alphonso olives, seeded and
   chopped
2 tablespoons drained capers,
   rinsed
2 tablespoons bitters or
   dry sherry
2 tablespoons extra-virgin olive oil
1 teaspoon fresh lemon thyme
¼ teaspoon fresh lemon zest
1 small clove garlic, crushed
freshly ground black pepper,
   to taste
lemon juice, to taste
36 crostini toasts (see page 61)

Place the bell peppers, olives,
capers, bitters, oil, thyme, lemon
zest, and garlic in a food processor.
Pulse the mixture until finely
chopped, then transfer to a
medium bowl. Season with
pepper and lemon juice. Spread
the tapenade on the crostini
and serve.

Yields 36 hor d'oeuvres

*Note: This tapenade can be stored in
the refrigerator for up to 1 week. Allow
refrigerated tapenade to reach room
temperature before serving.*

INCREDIBLY CHUNKY SALSA

This recipe for cooked salsa began its evolution during the very first harvest season after I moved to Colorado. The recipe has been altered and refined many times over the years, yet the salsa remains stable in flavor and resonance. It takes some time and effort, but the results are worth the work. The salsa retains its color and flavor well over several months in the pantry, and it makes a lively gift for the holiday season. My brother always asks for this salsa for Christmas. ∽ While this salsa serves well as an appetizer, I also use it as a sauce for a variety of baked dishes. It's also delicious warmed and served over scrambled eggs and topped with grated sharp cheddar.

HEAT SCALE: *medium*
BEST USE: *fresh or canned*

12 Anaheim chiles, roasted, peeled, seeded, deveined, and chopped
8 hot banana peppers, roasted, peeled, seeded, deveined, and chopped
2 yellow bell peppers, seeded and chopped
2 red bell peppers, seeded and chopped
1 purple bell pepper, seeded and chopped
5 serrano chiles, seeded, deveined, and chopped
1 large white onion, diced
3 tablespoons cumin
1½ teaspoons ground cinnamon
¼ teaspoon ground red pepper
1½ teaspoons coarsely ground New Mexico chile
two 28-ounce cans crushed tomatoes
28 ounces water
1 teaspoon sugar
2 tablespoons salt
¼ cup cider vinegar
1 cup chopped fresh cilantro
juice of 2 lemons

Process the Anaheim chiles and banana peppers in a blender. Place the bell peppers, serrano chiles, onions, cumin, cinnamon, red pepper, and New Mexico chile in a large, deep roaster or Dutch oven. Add the processed Anaheim chiles and banana peppers, crushed tomatoes, water, sugar, salt, and vinegar.

Cook the mixture over low heat about 30 minutes, or until the liquid reduces about 1 inch. Remove the pan from the stove.

Add the cilantro and the lemon juice. Mix well.

Cover the roaster with cheese-cloth and refrigerate overnight to let the flavors develop.

The next day, cook the salsa over medium heat 20-30 minutes, or until bubbling hot. Allow it to cool to warm before serving.

If canning, spoon the hot salsa into hot, sterilized jars, leaving ¼-inch headspace. Screw the lids and rings tightly on the jars, and process 20 minutes in a boiling-water bath. Remove the jars from the water and let stand in a draft-free area until the lids have popped.

Yields 6 pints

Note: This recipe takes 2 days to make.

BRUSCHETTA WITH GARLIC AND PEPPERS

This combination of olives, peppers, basil,
and balsamic vinegar provides an appetizer that pleases the palate
as well as the nose. I like to serve this with a platter of Asiago, provolone, and fresh
tomatoes for a summer lunch or light supper. Combine this appetizer
with a simple pasta and a salad for a more substantial
meal that's easy to make and satisfying.

HEAT SCALE: *mild*
BEST USE: *fresh*

Toasts
1 loaf crusty white Italian bread
2 cloves garlic, minced
¼ cup extra-virgin olive oil

Topping
½ cup Cerignola green olives,
*   pitted and chopped*
1 red or yellow bell pepper,
*   roasted, peeled, seeded, and*
*   chopped*
4 tablespoons extra-virgin olive oil
½-1 teaspoon ground red
*   pepper*
¼ cup chopped fresh basil
1 tablespoon balsamic vinegar
2 cloves garlic, crushed

For the toasts, preheat the broiler.
Cut the bread in half lengthwise. Then cut each half into slices, ¾ inch thick. Put the slices on a baking sheet. Broil about 6 inches from the heat, 3-5 minutes, or until the slices are a nutty brown. Turn the slices and broil the other side. Remove from the oven.

Mix the garlic and oil in a small bowl, and lightly brush the mixture on the slices while they are still warm.

For the topping, mix all of the topping ingredients in a medium bowl. Spoon a bit onto each warm bruschetta toast and serve immediately.

Yields 36 bruschetta toasts

Note: The bread can also be toasted over an open flame, but I recommend using the broiler for a large batch. The toasts store well in an air-tight container for 2-3 weeks. The topping can be made a day ahead, but warm it to room temperature before serving.

Bruschetta with Garlic and Peppers
(recipe this page)

CHINESE STEAMED BUNS

China is a country whose people have accomplished a vast array of distinct flavor combinations. Regardless of the province, the cuisine fills the kitchen with the scents of anise, garlic, chile, and soy. This recipe for steamed buns still stands as a favorite at my house. It was inspired by the steamed buns recipe found in Chinese Cooking *by Lee To Chun.* ∽ *This recipe calls for roast pork, which can be cooked, shredded, and stored in the refrigerator for up to a week. This cuts down on the assembly time of the buns considerably, yet it still takes an afternoon to make the yeast dough, allow it to rise, fill it, and steam it. These buns can be frozen or made 3-4 hours before steaming.*

HEAT SCALE: **medium**
BEST USE: **fresh or frozen**

Roast Pork
2 tablespoons soy sauce
2 tablespoons sweet sherry
1 tablespoon crushed garlic
½ teaspoon freshly ground
  black pepper
1 teaspoon ground ginger
½ teaspoon ground cinnamon
1 teaspoon ground star anise
one 1½-pound boneless pork
  roast

Filling
2 tablespoons peanut oil
4 scallions, green and white parts,
  minced
2 cloves garlic, crushed
1 Thai chile, dried and crushed, or
  ¼ teaspoon red pepper flakes
½ cup chopped green or purple
  bell peppers
2 cups minced roast pork
1 teaspoon sugar
3 tablespoons soy sauce
2 tablespoons sweet sherry
1½ tablespoons cornstarch
⅓ cup chicken broth

Dough
1 package dry yeast
1 tablespoon sugar
1¼ cups lukewarm water
3½-4 cups flour

For the roast pork, preheat the oven to 350°F.

In a medium bowl, combine the soy sauce, sherry, garlic, pepper, ginger, cinnamon, and star anise, and blend gently with a small whisk.

Rub the mixture onto all sides of the pork. Place the pork in an ovenproof baking dish and loosely cover it with aluminum foil. Roast the pork 40-45 minutes. Remove from the oven and set aside until cool. Mince or shred the pork, and store for future use or set aside to use for the filling.

For the filling, heat the oil in a wok or deep skillet over medium heat. Stir-fry the scallions and garlic 1 minute. Add the chiles, bell peppers, and pork, and stir-fry until the pork is heated through and the peppers are heated yet still firm. Blend in the sugar, soy sauce, and sherry, tossing well after each has been added. Dissolve the cornstarch in the broth, then add it to the pork mixture. Reduce the heat to medium-low, stirring continually until the mixture thickens. Remove the wok from the heat and set aside to cool. Transfer the mixture to a medium bowl and refrigerate until 30 minutes before assembly.

For the dough, sprinkle the yeast and sugar over the water in a medium bowl. Gently stir with a whisk until dissolved. Let the yeast mixture sit 15-20 minutes, or until a layer of foam forms on the surface. Add the flour 1 cup at a time until the entire amount has been worked into a soft dough. Turn the dough out onto a floured board or work surface and knead it 7-10 minutes until the dough becomes smooth and satiny. You may need to add a little additional flour to keep the dough from sticking to your hands and the work surface. Place the dough in a bowl brushed with peanut oil, cover with a towel, and let rise until the dough has doubled in bulk (1-1½ hours depending on the heat in your kitchen).

To assemble, punch the dough down and knead it on the floured surface 2-3 minutes. Roll it into a rope about 2 inches in diameter. Cut the dough into 24 equal pieces. Roll each piece into a circle about ⅛ inch thick and 3-3½ inches in diameter. Place a rounded teaspoon of filling in the center of each dough circle. Pull the sides of the dough up around the filling and pinch together at the top. Smooth out the dough and shape into rounded buns for steaming.

Place each bun on a small square piece of waxed paper, and cover all of the buns with a cloth, allowing them to rise about 30 minutes. Place the buns on their waxed paper in a steamer a few at a time, and steam 15-20 minutes, or until the buns are puffed, glossy, and smooth.

Yields 24 buns

Note: You can substitute 2 cups raw shrimp for the pork, as well as mixing 1 cup shrimp with 1 cup pork. When using half and half, add the shrimp to the stir-fry mix just before the cornstarch. Since the shrimp is chopped, it doesn't take more than 2 minutes to cook. It loses succulence and flavor if cooked any longer.

BLACK BEAN, PEPPER, AND LIME SALSA

*This is a cooked salsa that adds volume to fajitas and a variety
of tortilla and rice dishes. It can be canned and put into the pantry for colder
months when fresh Fresno chiles may not be available at your local market. Also try
it as an accompaniment to grilled tuna with rice seasoned with a dash of
cumin and grated queso fresco or hard Mexican table cheese.*

HEAT SCALE: **medium to
   medium-hot**
BEST USE: **fresh or canned**

1½ cups uncooked black beans
12 canned plum tomatoes,
   broiled, skinned, and seeded
1 large white onion, quartered or
   cut into chunks
1 green bell pepper, roasted,
   peeled, and seeded
2 yellow cubanelle peppers,
   roasted, peeled, and seeded
3 Fresno chiles
12 Anaheim chiles, roasted,
   peeled, and seeded
1 cup chopped fresh cilantro
2 teaspoons ground cinnamon
juice of ½ lemon
juice of 1 lime
1 tablespoon dried cumin
1 tablespoon coarsely ground
   tabasco chile, or ½ teaspoon
   red pepper flakes
2 tablespoons salt

Soak the beans overnight. Drain
and cook in a medium stockpot
over medium heat 1 hour, or until
tender. Refrigerate until ready
to use.

In a blender or food processor,
pulse the tomatoes, onions,
peppers, chiles, and cilantro until
chunky. Transfer to a deep roasting
pan, and cook over medium heat
15 minutes.

Add the cinnamon, lemon
juice, lime juice, cumin, tabasco
chile, salt, and black beans. Stir
until thoroughly blended.

Cook, stirring to avoid sticking,
20-25 minutes, or until the
mixture is bubbling hot. Serve
the salsa warm or at room
temperature.

If canning, pour hot into hot,
sterilized jars, leaving ¼-inch
headspace. Screw the lids and
rings tightly on the jars, and
process 20 minutes in a boiling-
water bath. Remove the jars
from the water and let stand in
a draft-free area until the lids
have popped.

Yields 6 half-pints

*Note: If not canned, this salsa stores
well in the refrigerator in an air-tight
container for 7-10 days.*

SAUCES

MIRASOL SAUCE

While this sauce serves well with a variety of tortilla dishes,
it also makes a succulent table sauce used for dipping or as a condiment
when combined with one large diced orange. Or add zest to breakfast or brunch by adding
it to eggs scrambled with sliced ripe olives and shredded Monterey Jack. I prefer to use the mirasol
dried, when its light scent of strawberry and its mild piquancy really
entertain the senses. These bright, cherry-red peppers retain
their color and shape even when dried.

HEAT SCALE: *hot*
BEST USE: *fresh or canned*

6 medium tomatoes, pricked,
   broiled, cored, peeled, and
   seeded
2 red bell peppers, roasted,
   peeled, and seeded
2 dried mirasol chiles, seeded
   and crushed
½ cup minced fresh cilantro
1 tablespoon salt
1 teaspoon dried cumin
½ cup lime juice

Process the tomatoes, bell peppers, chiles, cilantro, salt, and cumin in a blender. Transfer to a medium saucepan and cook over medium heat about 30 minutes, or until bubbling hot. Add the lime juice, stirring evenly throughout the mixture. Allow the mixture to return to a boil.

Serve fresh or pour into hot, sterilized jars, leaving ¼-inch headspace. Screw the lids and rings tightly on the jars, and process 20 minutes in a boiling-water bath. Remove the jars from the water and let stand in a draft-free area until the lids have popped.

Yields 2 pints

Note: This sauce serves well over cheese enchiladas or chicken or pork tacos.

top: Mirasol Sauce (recipe this page);
bottom: Orange Habanero Sauce
(recipe on page 84)

MARINARA PIZZA SAUCE

*A well-prepared pizza is one that appeals to your individual
requirements: thin, thick, crispy, or chewy. Of the many types of sauce spread onto
the dough, I like marinara the best. Marinara refers to sauce prepared sailor style, or with olive oil
and herbs but no cheese.* ✍ *Marinara sauce has become the traditional sauce for pizza and provides a flavor
base compatible with just about any topping you select. This sauce given here is best when the tomatoes
and peppers are plump with flavor and the garlic is bursting with aroma. I sometimes make it
with extra-virgin olive oil if I want a more intense flavor.*

HEAT SCALE: *mild*
BEST USE: *canned or fresh*

5-6 pounds ripe tomatoes,
  chopped
2 purple or red bell peppers,
  chopped
1 cayenne chile, or 1½ teaspoons
  red pepper flakes
½ cup sugar
3 tablespoons salt
½ cup fresh oregano
5 cloves garlic, chopped

Combine all of the ingredients in
a large saucepan and simmer over
medium-low heat 35-45 minutes,
or until bubbly. As the mixture
thickens, stir to prevent sticking.

When it has reached the desired
thickness, pour into hot, sterilized
jars, leaving ¼-inch headspace.
Screw the lids and rings tightly on
the jars, and process 20 minutes in

a boiling-water bath. Remove the
jars from the water and let stand
in a draft-free area until the lids
have popped.

Yields 5 pints

*Note: This sauce is also delicious
fresh. Just make it 8 hours or a day
before serving.*

OUTRAGEOUS GREEN CHILE SAUCE

*I often serve this sauce with chicken or vegetable enchiladas,
as well as with open-face tostadas layered with roasted poblano chiles, roasted red bell
peppers, sour cream, and diced plum tomatoes. ∽ Since this recipe calls for 25 pounds,
or about 1 bushel, of peppers, all of which need to be roasted, be sure to plan ahead. If you roast
the chiles yourself, you will need a morning or an afternoon for the entire process. The roasted chiles
need to be placed in plastic bags, cooled, peeled, seeded, and cut into strips or chopped.
Buying roasted chiles at an outdoor market saves time. You can purchase
your bushel, and you need only to let the peppers cool for cleaning.*

HEAT SCALE: *medium*
BEST USE: *canned or fresh*

25 pounds Anaheim chiles,
   roasted, peeled, seeded,
   and puréed
1 pound jalapeño chiles, seeded
   and chopped
2 cups chopped fresh cilantro
½ cup lime juice
2 tablespoons salt
2 tablespoons ground cumin

Combine all of the ingredients in a large bowl, then process in a blender in batches. (You may need to cook this in batches also.) Place the mixture in a large stockpot, and cook over medium-high heat about 45 minutes, or until thickened.

When boiling hot, pour into hot, sterilized jars, leaving ¼-inch headspace. Screw the lids and rings tightly on the jars, and process 20 minutes in a boiling-water bath. Remove the jars from the water and let stand in a draft-free area until the lids have popped.

Yields 7-9 quarts

Note: This sauce can also be served fresh.

PEPPER-LEMON CREAM SAUCE

*This colorful sauce adds elegance and palate-cleansing zest
to pasta and rice dishes. I have also tried this sauce with grilled chicken
and turkey breasts, as well as with steamed broccoli, mushrooms, and green beans
for a lighter, less-filling meal. Use this sauce to highlight and accent
food, as opposed to drowning it. A little goes a long way.*

HEAT SCALE: **mild**
BEST USE: **fresh or frozen**

1 cup heavy cream
¼ cup butter
zest of 2 lemons
½ cup grated Parmesan cheese
½ cup grated Romano cheese
2 yellow or orange bell peppers
   or cubanelle peppers, roasted,
   peeled, seeded, and diced
2 tablespoons minced fresh lemon
   thyme, optional
freshly ground white pepper,
   to taste

In a small saucepan, heat the
cream, butter, lemon zest, and
cheeses over medium-low heat
until the mixture is heated
through but not boiling. Add the
peppers. Cook on low heat
5 minutes. Add the lemon thyme,
if desired. Season with white
pepper.

Remove from the heat, let
cool 1-2 minutes, then serve or
pour into a storage container.

Yields 2 cups

*Note: To lower the fat content in the
sauce, use ½ cup milk and ½ cup
heavy cream. This sauce can be kept
in the refrigerator for 1 week or in the
freezer for 3 months.*

RED AND YELLOW
PASTA SAUCE

*This sauce transforms just about any pasta
into a colorful and warming feast when served with fresh
garlic bread and a plate of tomatoes and Lugano olives dressed with a little
olive oil, purple basil, and balsamic vinegar. It also works well
with mastaciolli, penne, or rigatoni.*

HEAT SCALE: *mild*
BEST USE: *fresh or frozen*

2 red bell peppers
1 yellow bell pepper
⅔ cup fresh basil
2 tablespoons olive oil
5 cloves garlic, chopped
1 cup yellow or orange tomatoes,
    broiled, seeded, and puréed
    but still chunky
salt, to taste
1 pound mastaciolli, penne, or
    rigatoni, cooked and drained
½ cup freshly grated Parmigiano-
    Reggiano cheese

Remove the stems, seeds, and veins from the peppers. Cut the peppers into lengthwise strips and set aside.

Rinse the basil and gently pat it dry. Cut or tear the leaves into small pieces. Set aside.

In a large frying pan, heat the oil over medium heat. Sauté the garlic to flavor the oil. Remove the garlic from the pan once it turns light brown. Add the peppers and cook over medium heat 10 minutes, or just until tender. Add the basil and tomato purée. Season with salt. Serve hot with the pasta. Toss with the cheese just before serving.

Yields 2+ cups

Note: This sauce keeps in the freezer for 4-6 weeks. If freezing, leave the pasta a bit firm, then drain it well. Allow the sauce to reach room temperature before adding it to the pasta. Seal in air-tight containers.

PEPPER AÏOLI

*The Provence region of France is home to a cache of recipes
redolent with herbs and spices. Aïoli is one of these, and Le Grande Aïoli
is probably one of the best-known cod dishes from that region. But aïoli is also
a garlic dip that can be used with raw vegetables. This recipe is
a variation that includes roasted yellow peppers.*

HEAT SCALE: **mild**
BEST USE: **fresh**

1 yellow bell pepper, roasted,
    peeled, and seeded
8 cloves garlic
4 egg yolks
1½ cups extra-virgin olive oil
3 teaspoons Dijon mustard
salt, to taste
freshly ground white pepper,
    to taste
lemon juice, to taste

In a blender, purée the pepper.
Remove the purée from the
blender. Purée the garlic. Add the
egg yolks and blend until smooth.
Add the oil gradually until
blended. Add the mustard. Season
with salt, white pepper, and lemon
juice. Add the pepper purée back
into the blender and process.

Yields 2 cups

*Note: This is good served with raw
tomatoes, mushrooms, celery, carrots,
cauliflower, and ripe olives.*

Pepper Aïoli (recipe this page)

ORANGE HABANERO SAUCE

*The golden habanero chile glows with color and possesses enough heat
to scald your tongue! When handling this fiery friend from the Yucatan, wear
gloves. This sauce makes an aromatic and delicious addition to any dish requiring hot sauce.
It is excellent for spicy spareribs or chicken. Attempting to use this as a table sauce
marks an element of true courage—or a death wish! (Photo on page 76.)*

HEAT SCALE: **hot**
BEST USE: **fresh or frozen**

2 tablespoons finely chopped
   golden orange habanero chiles
1 jalapeño chile, finely chopped
½ orange bell pepper, finely
   chopped
¼ cup minced onions
½ cup chopped yellow tomatoes
⅓ cup mandarine orange/
   tangerine juice or orange juice
¼ cup chopped fresh cilantro
juice from ½ lime
salt, to taste

Combine the chiles, bell peppers,
onions, and tomatoes in a medium
bowl. Add the orange/tangerine
juice, cilantro, and lime juice.
Season with salt. Serve fresh or
store tightly covered in the
refrigerator for up to 10 days.

Yields 1¾ cup

*Note: This sauce also freezes well for
up to 3 months.*

YELLOW PEPPER TOMATO SAUCE

*This sauce graces spinach pasta with ease and adds
a pleasant diversion to cheese ravioli or cannelloni. The
peppers, yellow tomatoes, and nutmeg blend mellow intensity with
spice and provide contrast to cheese and pasta. Embellish this sauce with freshly
chopped Genovese basil for additional flavor. When prepared with the
basil, the sauce can be served warm along with a plate of
crostini or raw mushrooms for dipping.*

HEAT SCALE: **mild**
BEST USE: **fresh**

1 tablespoon olive oil
2 yellow tomatoes, chopped
2 yellow Hungarian sweet
   peppers, seeded and chopped
2½ tablespoons butter
3 tablespoons flour
1½ cups milk
½ cup light cream
1 tablespoon tomato paste
salt, to taste
freshly ground white pepper,
   to taste
freshly grated nutmeg, to taste

In a large frying pan, heat the oil over medium heat. Sauté the tomatoes and peppers until most of the liquid has evaporated. Set aside.

Melt the butter in a medium saucepan over medium-low heat. Stir in the flour and cook, stirring, 2 minutes. Remove from the heat and pour in the milk, beating vigorously with a whisk to blend. Return to the heat and continue stirring until the sauce comes to a boil. Add the cream and tomato paste, stirring thoroughly. Add the tomatoes and peppers and simmer 2 minutes. Season with salt, white pepper, and nutmeg.

Yields 3 cups

PERUVIAN HOT SAUCE

*There are many variations of Peruvian hot sauce. The combination
of brown sugar, cayenne, and cinnamon lends a spicy, hot sweetness to pork,
fish, beans, and rice. I often use it as a marinade for grilling, and I use additional sauce on
the table when serving. Its voluminous flavor is a welcome pantry treat on cold winter
days. It adds dimension to a lunch of sliced apples, corn bread, and a salad of
greens tossed with olive oil, lime juice, and diced mild cheddar.*

HEAT SCALE: **medium-hot**
BEST USE: **fresh or canned**

24 large ripe tomatoes, chopped
3 medium Jonathan apples,
   chopped
3 large onions, chopped
3 green bell peppers, seeded
   and chopped
3 jalapeño chiles, seeded,
   deveined, and chopped
1 cayenne chile, or 3 teaspoons
   ground red pepper
3 cloves garlic, minced
3 cups loosely packed brown
   sugar
1 tablespoon allspice
1 teaspoon ground cinnamon
1 tablespoon salt
1 cup white wine vinegar

Combine the tomatoes, apples,
onions, bell peppers, chiles, garlic,
and brown sugar in a medium
saucepan. Simmer 1 hour over
medium heat. Stir frequently to
prevent sticking. Add the allspice,
cinnamon, salt, and vinegar. Cook
20-30 minutes, or until the
mixture reaches the desired
thickness and is boiling.

Serve fresh or pour into hot,
sterilized jars, leaving ¼-inch
headspace. Screw the lids and
rings tightly on the jars, and
process 15 minutes in a boiling-
water bath. Remove the jars from
the water and let stand in a
draft-free area until the lids
have popped.

Yields 6 pints

CHILE TEQUILA BARBECUE SAUCE

*This combination of citrus, chiles, and tequila is a wonderful accent
to lamb, poultry, pork, and seafood for the grill. It is inspired by the many
flavor combinations that come from the recipes and research of Diana Kennedy
in* The Regional Cooks of Mexico *and* The Cuisines of Mexico. *I like to blend this
sauce with cottage cheese or sour cream and serve it wrapped in warm
corn tortillas that have been rubbed with a little fresh lime juice.*

HEAT SCALE: **mild to medium**
BEST USE: **fresh or frozen**

½ cup peanut oil
6 pasilla chiles
2 dried mirasol chiles, crushed
1 cup orange juice
½ teaspoon salt
1 small onion, diced
⅓ cup tequila
1 tablespoon dried cilantro

In a large frying pan, heat the oil over medium heat. Sauté the chiles with their stems intact, until slightly soft. Remove the chiles from the pan, but leave the oil. Set the chiles aside to cool. Remove the stems, skins, and seeds once the chiles are cool enough to handle.

In a blender or food processor, purée the chiles, orange juice, and salt into a smooth sauce. Set aside.

In the oil in the frying pan, sauté the onions until they're soft and translucent. Add the sauce, and cook over medium heat 5 minutes. Set the sauce aside to cool. Blend in the tequila with a whisk, add the cilantro, and serve.

Yields 1½-2 cups

Note: If freezing, pour the sauce into a glass or plastic freezer container. It can be stored for 2-3 months.

SALADS & SIDE DISHES

top: Tomato, Orange, and Pepper Soup
(recipe on page 119);
bottom: Mixed Pepper Salad (recipe on page 90)

MIXED PEPPER SALAD

*This salad is good for a lunch or summer supper
when guests grace your table. The salad and its dressing can be
prepared in advance and blended just before serving. It can be topped with grilled tuna,
shrimp, or chicken for a heartier main dish and served along with a chilled soup, bread, and sliced
Asiago or mozzarella. Or enjoy this dish with a plate of crusty bread,
sliced fresh pears, and Stilton cheese. (Photo on page 88.)*

HEAT SCALE: **mild**
BEST USE: **fresh**

Dressing
¼ cup finely chopped fresh
　oregano
2 teaspoons finely chopped
　fresh thyme
¼ cup freshly grated Parmigiano-
　Reggiano cheese
½ cup extra-virgin olive oil
¼ cup balsamic vinegar

Salad
1 red bell pepper, seeded
1 yellow bell pepper, seeded
1 purple bell pepper, seeded
1 orange bell pepper, seeded
2 cups romaine lettuce
2 cups mesclun greens
2 cups butterhead lettuce
1 clove garlic
½ cup chopped reconstituted
　yellow sun-dried tomatoes,
　or ½ cup diced fresh yellow
　tomatoes
salt and freshly ground white
　pepper, to taste
niçoise olives, optional
toasted hazelnuts, optional
croutons, optional

For the dressing, in a screw-top jar
or blender, combine the oregano,
thyme, cheese, oil, and vinegar
until just blended. Set aside.

For the salad, slice the peppers
lengthwise into ¼-inch-wide
strips. Wash and drain the salad
greens in a colander and dry well.

Place the mixed greens in a
large wooden bowl that has been
rubbed with the garlic clove. Add
the pepper strips and yellow
tomatoes and toss. Add the
dressing and toss lightly. Season
with salt and pepper.

Add olives, toasted hazelnuts,
and croutons, if desired.

Serves 8

MIXED GRILL

*The color combination achieved by mixing and grilling
vegetables is itself a celebration. The aubergine eggplant enhances the
green zucchini and chiles. All dance in lively contrast to the bright crimson tomatoes
and glowing orange bell peppers. The medley is complete with the creamy glow of garlic, slightly
toasty around the edges. Be sure to avoid overcooking the vegetables—they really
don't take long, and the lovely colors turn to ebony if the vegetables
overstay their position on a hot grill. (Photo on page 92.)*

HEAT SCALE: **medium**
BEST USE: **fresh**

Dressing
3 leaves green basil
3 leaves opal basil
1 jalapeño or Fresno chile, seeded
   and deveined
1 cup extra-virgin olive oil
½ teaspoon salt

Vegetables
2½ teaspoons salt
8 slices peeled eggplant,
   ¼ inch thick
8 slices zucchini, ¼ inch thick
8 medium plum tomatoes, halved
   lengthwise
8 cremini mushrooms
1 orange bell pepper, seeded
   and sliced lengthwise into
   1-inch-wide strips
8 cloves garlic, preferably
   elephant garlic
½ lemon or lime

For the dressing, combine the green basil, opal basil, chile, oil, and salt in a blender and process until smooth. Transfer to a small bowl and set aside.

For the vegetables, sprinkle the salt over the eggplant. Squeeze the eggplant gently to remove any liquid. Place the eggplant, zucchini, tomatoes, mushrooms, and bell peppers on a plate.

Oil a piece of aluminum foil and wrap the garlic in it. Place the garlic packet on the grill over high heat. Brush all of the vegetables with half of the dressing. Grill the vegetables a few at a time. (It takes about 15 minutes to grill everything; the garlic should stay on the grill the entire time to become tender.)

Return the grilled vegetables to the plate and drizzle with the remaining dressing. Squeeze lime or lemon juice over the vegetables before serving.

Serve warm or cold.

Serves 6-8

TUNA-PEPPER SALAD

*Fresh tuna that has been steamed or grilled
and then flaked for salad tastes nothing like its canned cousin
found at the market. While this fish isn't always available fresh, this salad will
make the most of it when it's in season. This is an excellent luncheon dish that can be
prepared in advance for guests. Sliced oranges, tangerines, and seedless red grapes
complement the tuna, pepper, and herb medley with a tangy sweetness
and contrast. Add 2 cups of cooked tomato or
spinach penne for a heartier dish.*

HEAT SCALE: **mild**
BEST USE: **fresh**

one 8-ounce tuna steak, grilled
    and cooled
1 orange or red bell pepper,
    finely chopped
1 cup seeded and finely chopped
    green Cerignola or other olives
4 stalks celery, diced
1 tablespoon minced fresh chives
2 tablespoons minced fresh
    tarragon
¼ cup extra-virgin olive oil
1 teaspoon white wine vinegar
salt and freshly ground black
    pepper, to taste

Place the tuna in a large bowl and
gently break it into chunky flakes
with a fork.

Add the peppers, olives, and
celery and toss. Blend in the
chives and tarragon. Add the oil
and vinegar and blend into the
salad with the fork to coat all of
the ingredients. Season with salt
and pepper.

Serves 6-8

*Note: This salad stores well in the
refrigerator for 2-3 days.*

PEPPER AND TOMATO SALAD

*This salad should be made 1 hour
ahead and refrigerated, but allowed to warm to room
temperature for 15 minutes before serving. I serve it with thick slices of toasted
homemade wheat bread and Alphonso olives dressed with olive
oil and fresh oregano. (Photo on page 136.)*

HEAT SCALE: *mild*
BEST USE: *fresh*

*2 medium tomatoes, each cut
    into 3 or 4 slices*
*4 ounces whole-milk mozzarella
    cheese, cut into ⅛-inch-thick
    slices*
*1 red bell pepper, roasted,
    peeled, seeded, and chopped*
¼ cup drained capers, rinsed
¼ cup extra-virgin olive oil
3 tablespoons balsamic vinegar
6-8 large opal basil leaves

Place the tomatoes on a platter in
a single layer or in a slightly overlapping format. Place a slice of
mozzarella on each tomato. Place
a spoonful of chopped peppers on
each slice of mozzarella. Sprinkle
the capers liberally over the
entire salad.

Drizzle the oil, then the vinegar
over the salad. Top each tomato
slice with a basil leaf.

Serves 6-8

WHITE BEANS WITH ORANGE PEPPERS

I traditionally use cannellini beans when cooking with peppers, pasta, and citrus fruits. However, you can substitute bolitas or small or medium navy beans. It's easy to make a batch of beans 1 or 2 days in advance and keep them in the refrigerator. The peppers and the rest of the ingredients can be added close to mealtime, preserving the freshness and flavor of the orange bell pepper and the seasonings.

HEAT SCALE: *mild to medium*
BEST USE: *fresh*

4 ounces dried cannellini beans,
    soaked overnight
4 tablespoons virgin olive oil
2 orange bell peppers, seeded
    and coarsely chopped
½ medium onion, diced
¼ cup chicken broth
juice of 1 lemon
½-1 teaspoon freshly ground
    white pepper
Parmigiano-Reggiano cheese,
    to taste

In a medium saucepan over medium heat, simmer the beans in water to cover by 2 inches until tender, about 45 minutes.

While the beans are cooking, heat the oil in a large frying pan over medium heat. Sauté the peppers and onions until tender but still slightly firm. Add the chicken broth and cook over medium heat 5 minutes. Add the lemon juice and white pepper, cooking another 5 minutes.

When the beans are tender, remove them from the heat, drain them, and transfer them to a warmed platter. Cover with the pepper mixture, and sprinkle the cheese on top.

Serves 4

HARVEST PIE

Italian cooks in my family have their own recipes for harvest pie.
Some like to make a pie from green and red peppers, using small, fluted
tart pans for individual servings. Others make a large round pie, using yellow peppers,
Genovese basil, and pine nuts. I have even experimented with a layer of ricotta-egg mixture beneath
the peppers. This recipe is still my favorite. It combines enough but not too many flavors,
and it remains ever so slightly piquant. I have used it as a lunch entrée
as well as an accompaniment to a heartier main course.

HEAT SCALE: *medium*
BEST USE: *fresh*

Crust
3 cups bread flour
4 ounces butter, chipped
2-3 tablespoons vegetable
　shortening
½ teaspoon salt
4-5 tablespoons water

Filling
4 tablespoons olive oil
2 medium onions, diced
4 plum tomatoes, seeded and
　chopped
½ cup sun-dried tomatoes, not
　packed in oil, snipped coarsely
1 red bell pepper, seeded and
　chopped
2 orange bell peppers, seeded
　and chopped
1 yellow bell pepper, seeded
　and chopped
1 tablespoon fresh oregano
1 tablespoon salt
1 teaspoon freshly ground
　white pepper
dash of ground cinnamon
¾ cup grated Asiago cheese,
　garnish

For the crust, sift the flour and transfer to a flat, preferably marble work surface. Make a well in the middle of the mound. Add the butter, shortening, and salt, gradually working them into the flour with your fingers. Add the water, half at a time, and knead the dough until smooth. Cover with plastic wrap and set aside.

For the filling, preheat the oven to 350°F. In a large frying pan, heat the oil over medium heat. Sauté the onions 15 minutes, or until translucent. Add the tomatoes and peppers. Cook over low heat 20 minutes, stirring frequently. Pour all of the liquid out of the frying pan. Then add the oregano, salt, white pepper, and cinnamon, mixing well. Set aside.

To assemble, roll out the dough to ¼ inch thick. Line a buttered, 10-inch springform pan with the dough, going up the sides 1½-2 inches. Place the pepper mixture on top of the dough. Bake 35-40 minutes.

Remove the pie from oven and let sit 1-2 minutes. Release the pan from the pie. Garnish with the Asiago and serve.

Serves 8-10

Harvest Pie (recipe this page)

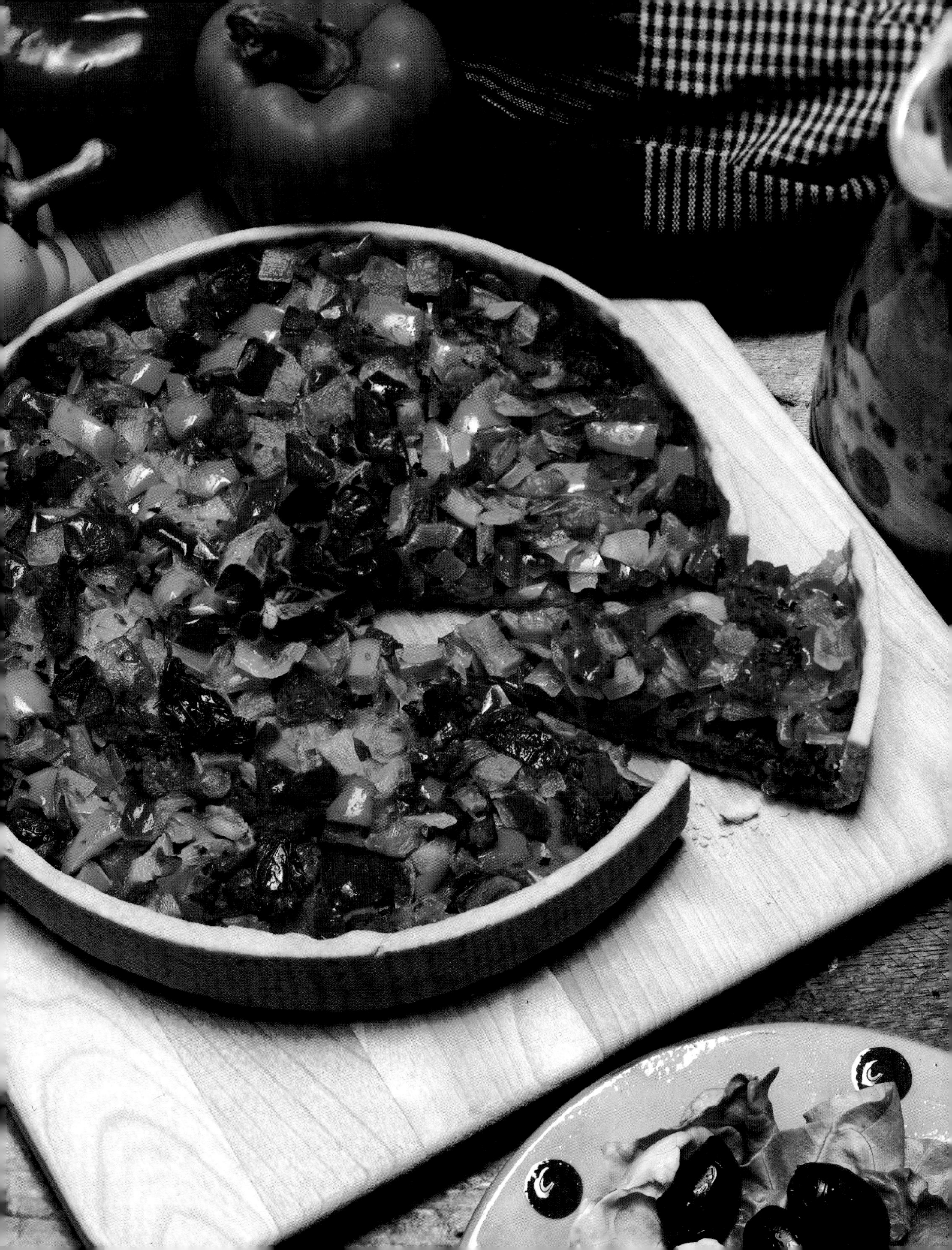

BAKED PEPPERS

*Baked peppers are easy to make
and exemplify Italy's love of cooking vegetables
simply with olive oil, garlic, and a little spice. A dash of balsamic
vinegar adds a lively flavor to this dish. While the peppers burst
with their best flavor during the harvest seasons, this dish
warms the soul during colder winter months.*

HEAT SCALE: **mild**
BEST USE: **fresh**

1 large red bell pepper, seeded
    and quartered lengthwise
2 large green bell peppers,
    seeded and quartered
    lengthwise
2 large yellow bell peppers,
    seeded and quartered
    lengthwise
4 large cloves garlic, crushed
¾ cup chopped fresh parsley
½ cup olive oil
salt and freshly ground black
    pepper, to taste
3 tablespoons balsamic vinegar

Preheat the oven to 400°F. Alternating the colors of the peppers, place them cut side up in an oiled 9-inch by 12-inch baking dish. Mix the garlic, parsley, and oil in a medium bowl. Spoon the mixture over the peppers. Season with salt and pepper.

Cover lightly with foil and bake 30 minutes, or until the peppers are tender and the undersides are lightly browned. Transfer to a serving platter. Sprinkle the vinegar over the peppers. Serve at room temperature.

Serves 6-8

STUFFED TOMATOES

While Thomas Jefferson's vegetable garden yielded spectacular produce, the red and yellow tomatoes he was so fond of in the 1780s found a chilly reception throughout other areas of the United States. Then the tide began to turn during the late 19th century. Henry Heinz created ketchup. Later on, Joseph Campbell and Abraham Anderson began canning beefsteak tomatoes, and Campbell went on to develop his famous tomato soup. ⌒ *This recipe combines tomatoes, peppers, herbs, and cheese for a grilled treat. Beefsteak tomatoes or your favorite meaty variety retain texture despite the heat. Use plum tomatoes if you want to try this dish as an appetizer.*

HEAT SCALE: *medium*
BEST USE: *fresh*

3 large, firm tomatoes
2 Fresno chiles, seeded,
    deveined, and minced
2 cloves garlic, minced
3 tablespoons chopped
    fresh parsley
¼ teaspoon dried epazote
3 tablespoons olive oil
¾ cup grated Muenster cheese

Cut the tomatoes in half lengthwise and remove the seeds. Scoop out some of the pulp and transfer it to a small bowl. The tomato shells should look like small bowls, ready to hold their filling.

Combine the pulp with the chiles, garlic, parsley, *epazote*, oil, and cheese. Stuff the tomatoes with the mixture. Top with additional grated cheese, if desired. Put a loose foil tent over the tomatoes and grill over medium-hot temperature about 10 minutes. They are ready to serve when the cheese begins to bubble.

Serves 6

PEPPERS, OLIVES, MUSHROOMS, AND ZUCCHINI

*The cremini mushrooms used in this recipe add volume
and contrast to the mellow zucchini, savory peppers, and slightly
tangy Alphonso olives. This dish is good as a topping for pasta. I like it
with tomato angel hair pasta and a spoonful of ricotta cheese,
warmed to room temperature, on the side.*

HEAT SCALE: *mild*
BEST USE: *fresh*

¼ cup olive oil
2 cloves garlic, crushed
1 orange bell pepper, seeded and
    cut into ½-inch-wide strips
1½ cups sliced zucchini
1 cup cremini mushrooms, sliced
    into thirds
½ cup whole Alphonso olives
1 teaspoon dried oregano
fresh rosemary, to taste
pinch of fresh mint
juice of ½ lemon

In a large frying pan, heat the oil
over medium heat. Sauté the
garlic until golden. Add the
peppers and sauté until slightly
soft. Add the zucchini and cook
another 2-3 minutes, or until
tender. Add the mushrooms
and olives, and cook another
3-5 minutes. Add the herbs and

lemon juice. Toss and remove
from the heat. Serve immediately.

Yields 2½ cups

*Note: Porcini mushrooms can be
substituted for creminis to create a
meatier dish, or try a blend of your
favorite wild mushrooms. I suggest
reducing the zucchini by ½ cup when
using the porcini or wild-mix
mushrooms.*

PAN-ROASTED PEPPERS

*Pan-roasted peppers are made at my house on a weekly basis
and are kept in the refrigerator or eaten immediately. They are simple
to make and can be easily added to many other recipes or made to accompany a plate
of risotto or cheese, bread, and salad. I roast green peppers, as well as orange, red, yellow, and purple.
Most sweet and many hot peppers lend themselves to roasting. Each has its own flavor
and blends well with different herb mixes, but I combine the peppers with
the ingredients here more frequently than with others.*

HEAT SCALE: *mild*
BEST USE: *fresh or canned*

⅓ cup extra-virgin olive oil
6 large green or red Italian
   or Hungarian sweet peppers,
   seeded and halved lengthwise
salt and freshly ground black
   pepper, to taste
½ cup toasted pine nuts
½ cup freshly chopped parsley
½ cup balsamic vinegar
1 tablespoon minced lemon
   thyme
1 clove garlic

In a large frying pan, heat the oil over low heat. Sauté the peppers very slowly, 20-30 minutes. Turn the peppers occasionally to make sure that they are cooked on all sides. Season with salt and pepper.

While the peppers are cooking, blend the pine nuts and parsley in a small bowl and set aside.

Add the vinegar and thyme to the frying pan. Turn each pepper one more time, in order to pick up the scent and flavor of the vinegar.

Remove the peppers from the pan and transfer to a shallow wooden bowl rubbed with the garlic clove. Top with the pine nuts and parsley. Season with a little more salt. Serve at once.

Serves 4-6

Note: If canning, place ½ teaspoon coarse sea salt in the bottom of a pint jar. Pack the peppers in the jar and add 1 clove garlic, pine nuts, and parsley. Pour in ½ cup to ¾ cup hot virgin olive oil, leaving ¼-inch head-space. Screw the lid and ring tightly on the jar, and process 15 minutes in a boiling-water bath. Remove the jar from the water and let stand in a draft-free area until the lid has popped.

BREADS

*Focaccia with Peppers and Parsley
(recipe on page 105)*

PIZZA WITH PEPPERS, GJETOST, AND SHRIMP

*It is highly unorthodox to mix cheese of any kind with fish.
However, this combination of gjetost cheese, mozzarella, and shrimp somehow works,
despite the fact that it does not follow the rules. (Photo on page 116.)*

HEAT SCALE: *mild*
BEST USE: *fresh*

Dough
1 cup warm water
½ teaspoon sugar
1 package dry yeast
3-4 cups bread flour
1 tablespoon salt
2 tablespoons butter, chipped
2-3 tablespoons olive oil

Topping
freshly ground black pepper,
   to taste
1 teaspoon garlic powder
1½ cups shredded mozzarella
   cheese
½ cup shredded gjetost cheese
12 medium shrimp, cleaned,
   coarsely chopped, and well
   drained
3 red bell peppers, roasted,
   peeled, seeded, and sliced
   lengthwise into ½-inch-wide
   strips

For the dough, place the water in a small bowl. Add the sugar and whisk until dissolved. Add the yeast, blending gently into the water with the whisk. Set aside in a warm place for 10 minutes. The yeast mixture should have a layer of foam on top.

In a large bowl, combine 3 cups of the flour with the salt and butter pieces. Blend the butter into the flour with your fingertips. Add the yeast mixture, blending it into the flour with a fork until enough liquid is absorbed so that the dough is ready to knead. Add more flour if necessary.

Beat the dough with a wooden spoon or knead it on a floured surface 10 minutes, adding flour if necessary. The dough should be smooth, shiny, and soft. Form it into a ball. Place the dough in an oiled bowl, turning it to coat it with oil, and cover with plastic wrap. Let the dough rise 45 minutes, or until it doubles in size.

Preheat the oven to 375°F.

Roll out the dough to a ⅜-inch thickness, and place in an oiled 17-inch by 11-inch by 1-inch pan, in a large round pan, or on a baking stone.

For the topping, sprinkle the dough with the pepper and garlic. Cover with the cheeses. Top with the shrimp and bell peppers.

Bake 20-25 minutes. Remove the pizza from the oven and serve immediately.

Serves 8-12

Note: Gjetost cheese comes from Norway and can be purchased in the deli section of many larger supermarkets, in ethnic food stores, or through most purveyors of imported cheese. This creamy, sweet goat cheese is caramel in color.

FOCACCIA WITH PEPPERS AND PARSLEY

*Focaccia lends itself to the use of a variety of herbs and ingredients
in addition to the peppers and parsley here. Focaccia ala Genovese calls for onions
sliced thin, sautéed in olive oil, and spread over the dough. Sage, rosemary, roasted garlic, and a
little mint also provide diversity. The cooks at the restaurant Diana in Bologna, Italy, add bits of quality
bacon into the dough. This recipe calls for no bacon but plenty of parsley, for a simple,
crisp bread that disappears quickly from the table. (Photo on page 102.)*

HEAT SCALE: *mild*
BEST USE: *fresh*

*pizza dough, 1 recipe
   (see page 104)*
¼ cup olive oil
⅓ cup cornmeal
*1 orange bell or 2 cubanelle
   peppers, seeded and diced*
*4 scallions, green and white parts,
   chopped*
*½ cup fresh Italian parsley,
   chopped*
*2 large sage leaves, finely
   chopped, or 1 tablespoon dried*
¾ cup grated Parmesan cheese
*freshly ground black pepper,
   to taste*

Prepare the pizza dough. Preheat the oven to 375°F. Oil a 15-inch by 10-inch by 1-inch pan and sprinkle with cornmeal. Place the dough evenly in the pan, pushing the dough with your fingers to the edges of the pan. Lightly brush the dough surface with oil. Top the dough with the peppers, scallions, parsley, and sage. Sprinkle with the cheese and season with pepper. Bake 30-45 minutes. Serve hot or at room temperature.

Serves 10-12

THE RED BELL, BOILED-EGG SANDWICH FROM FIRENZE

*Florence, like other Italian cities, abounds with small cafés where
you can purchase something light to eat all day long. Stalls offer a variety of sandwiches
that contain a seemingly unlikely yet delicious combination of ingredients. You'll find arugula, mezuna,
sliced boiled eggs, thin sheets of mozzarella, or dry ricotta gracefully adorned by any number of herbs.
The ingredients may sit on top of or within focaccia that looks like a small plate, or nestle inside split
loaves of different shapes and sizes, all covered with tangy and somewhat thick crusts. The
memory of those delightful sandwiches inspired the combination offered here.*

HEAT SCALE: *mild*
BEST USE: *fresh*

one 12-inch to 14-inch loaf Italian
  bread, sliced horizontally and
  then cut into 4 or 6 sections
½ cup olive oil
fresh lettuce, endive, or other
  greens, to taste
3 large yellow tomatoes, sliced
6 hard-boiled eggs, sliced
12 slices fresh mozzarella cheese
3 red bell peppers, roasted,
  peeled, seeded, and cut in
  half lengthwise
freshly ground white pepper,
  to taste
salt, to taste
balsamic vinegar, to taste

Brush the inside of the bread
lightly with the oil. On the
bottom slices of the bread, create
layers of greens, tomatoes, egg,
mozzarella, and red peppers.
Season with white pepper, salt,
and vinegar. Cap with the top
bread slices. Warm 10 minutes in
a 375°F oven or serve at room
temperature.

Serves 4-6

*top: Pepper Walnut Bread (recipe on page 109);
bottom: The Red Bell, Boiled-Egg
Sandwich from Firenze (recipe this page)*

PEPPER CORN MUFFINS

*The combination of jalapeño chiles and
golden raisins provides an unusual sweet yet hot contrast to
the texture and flavor of the corn. These muffins make good accompaniments
to fresh tomato soup garnished with opal basil or to fish grilled with sage and served with
a salad of greens tossed with oil and raspberry vinegar. Or try the muffins on
a wintry Saturday afternoon. Serve with honey butter and a pot
of almond herbal tea. (Photo on page 141.)*

HEAT SCALE: **medium**
BEST USE: **fresh or frozen**

2 cups buttermilk
2 eggs
½ cup sugar
⅓ cup melted butter or
    vegetable oil
2 cups yellow cornmeal
2 cups bread flour
4 teaspoons baking powder
1 teaspoon baking soda
1 teaspoon salt
3 jalapeño chiles, seeded,
    deveined, and diced
¾ cup golden raisins

Preheat the oven to 375°F.

In a medium bowl, whisk the buttermilk, eggs, sugar, and butter or oil. In a large bowl, stir together the cornmeal, flour, baking powder, baking soda, and salt with a fork. Add the liquids to the dry ingredients and mix just until blended. Do not beat. Stir in the chiles and raisins. Pour into lined muffin tins, and bake 20-30 minutes.

*Yields 12 large or
24 medium muffins*

Note: These muffins retain the best flavor when stored in the freezer for no more than 3 months. Store in air-tight plastic containers or in heavy-duty freezer bags.

PEPPER WALNUT BREAD

*Pepper walnut bread can be eaten alone or with soups
and salads, poultry and fish, or a platter of steamed broccoli, cauliflower,
and mushrooms garnished with roasted red bell peppers and scallions. I serve it with
tarragon chicken and mixed baby greens. It can be baked a few days ahead and reheated
for lunch guests, but it's best served fresh and slightly warm. While there
are many types of walnut bread, this variation is one I choose
to make again and again. (Photo on page 107.)*

HEAT SCALE: *mild*
BEST USE: *fresh or frozen*

1 package dry yeast
*¾ cup milk, at room
 temperature*
3-3¼ cups bread flour
*2 tablespoons chopped fresh
 rosemary*
1½ teaspoons salt
3 tablespoons peanut oil
*2 cups (16 ounces) chopped
 shelled walnuts*
*1 tablespoon finely chopped fresh
 oregano*
*1 Hungarian sweet gypsy or
 corno di toro pepper, seeded
 and diced*
olive oil
1 onion, thinly sliced

In a small bowl, dissolve the yeast in the milk. Allow it to rest in a draft-free spot about 20 minutes, or until it gets foamy.

Place the flour in a large bowl and make a well in the center. Add the rosemary, milk and yeast mixture, salt, and 2 tablespoons of the peanut oil into the well. Knead 15-20 minutes, or until the mixture becomes a soft, smooth dough. Add the walnuts, oregano, and peppers and knead a few more minutes to mix thoroughly (add ¼ cup more flour if necessary). Shape the dough into a ball, and rub it with a little olive oil. Place it in a bowl, cover it with plastic wrap, and set it aside in a warm place until the dough has doubled in volume, 45-60 minutes.

After the dough has risen, punch it down. Shape it into a 6-inch-diameter circle, 1½ inches thick, on a floured working surface. Place the dough in an oiled 8-inch round cake pan or on a baking stone, cover it, and allow it to rise, 30-45 minutes.

Preheat the oven to 400°F.

In a large frying pan, heat the remaining peanut oil over low heat, and sauté the onions until translucent. Remove the frying pan from the heat, and set aside to allow the onions to cool.

Once the dough has risen, cover it with the onions. Bake about 25 minutes. Allow it to cool, but slice while slightly warm.

Yields 1 loaf

*Note: Toasted filberts or almonds may
be substituted for the walnuts. I like
the combination of filberts with ¼ cup
of chopped fresh parsley. This bread
freezes and reheats well.*

THE YELLOW BELL SWISS SANDWICH

The yellow bell pepper glows with color before and
after it's roasted. Basil leaves, along with the cream cheese and Swiss cheese,
provide a delightful foil for the peppers and the bread. You'll want nothing but a glass
of wine or tea with this sandwich. It stands alone. This sandwich is also good with
a slight squeeze of lemon or a few drops of balsamic vinegar.

HEAT SCALE: *mild*
BEST USE: *fresh*

¼ cup extra-virgin olive oil
2 cloves garlic
4 large yellow bell peppers,
    peeled, seeded, and cut
    in half lengthwise
one 12-inch loaf crusty Italian
    or French bread, sliced
    horizontally and then cut into
    4 sections
4 ounces cream cheese, softened
salt and freshly ground black
    pepper, to taste
8 large opal basil leaves
4 ounces sliced Swiss cheese

Heat the oil in a large frying pan over medium heat. Add the garlic and peppers, cooking over medium-high heat until the pepper skins are toasty, 15-20 minutes. Remove the peppers and let cool. Discard the garlic or set aside for another use.

On the bottom slices of the bread, spread the cream cheese. Add two pieces of pepper to each. Season with salt and pepper. Add 2 leaves of basil to each. Add the Swiss cheese. Cap with the top bread slices. Serve slightly warmed or at room temperature.

Serves 4

SOUPS

SWEET PEPPER SOUP

*The roasted peppers in this recipe add dimension and
a mild, nutty flavor to the other ingredients. This soup can be made
a day in advance, and it retains excellent flavor when warmed. It complements
tossed green salad, steamed shrimp, and corn on the cob. Or try it
with bread and a small plate of sliced tomatoes.*

HEAT SCALE: **mild**
BEST USE: **fresh or frozen**

3 tablespoons olive oil
1 medium onion, chopped
3 large yellow bell peppers,
  seeded and chopped
2 large orange bell peppers, one
  seeded and chopped; one
  seeded and halved
¼ cup tubettini or small elbow
  macaroni
¼ teaspoon red pepper flakes
salt and freshly ground black
  pepper, to taste
2 tablespoons dry sherry
3-4 cups chicken broth
balsamic vinegar, to taste
10-12 fresh basil leaves, coarsely
  chopped

In a large saucepan, heat the oil over medium heat. Sauté the onions 3-4 minutes, or until translucent. Add the yellow peppers, chopped orange peppers, tubettini, red pepper flakes, salt, black pepper, sherry, and broth. Bring to a medium boil. Lower the heat and simmer 20 minutes, or until the tubettini is cooked. Be careful not to overcook the pasta.

While the soup is cooking, preheat the broiler. Place the halved orange peppers on a piece of aluminum foil, cut side down, 5 inches from the heat. Broil the peppers until all sides are black. Put the charred peppers in a plastic bag, let all the air escape, tie it closed, and let the peppers sit 20 minutes. When the peppers are cool enough to handle, peel or rub the skin from the peppers with your hands.

Transfer 2 cups of the cooked soup to a blender and process about 1 minute, or until smooth. Return the soup to the pot and heat through. Taste for seasoning, adding more salt and black pepper if desired. Serve the soup in individual bowls garnished with slices of the roasted peppers. Season with vinegar and basil.

Yields 6 cups; serves 4-6

Note: This soup can also be placed in a storage container and frozen.

SPICY CRAB SOUP

*A friend passed this recipe along to me two
decades ago when we were tag checkers at the beach
on Long Beach Island, N.J. Although the consistency of the broth has
undergone experimentation and the ingredients have at times expanded to include
rice or orzo, the flavor proves best with the original. This is a thin
yet flavorful broth enhanced by the combination of crab,
red bell peppers, and cream. (Photo on page 112.)*

HEAT SCALE: *mild*
BEST USE: *fresh*

2 cups fresh or defrosted frozen
   crabmeat
1 tablespoon unsalted butter
4 tablespoons dry sherry or
   marsala wine, at room
   temperature
1 teaspoon flour
1 quart whole milk
2 tablespoons onion juice
2 tablespoons freshly minced
   garlic
large pinch of freshly ground
   white pepper
½ teaspoon Worcestershire sauce
salt, to taste
⅔ cup chopped red bell peppers
½ cup heavy cream, whipped
dash of nutmeg, optional
½ cup finely chopped fresh
   parsley, garnish

Remove all cartilage and pieces of shell from the crabmeat. Simmer water in the lower portion of a double boiler; in the top portion, melt the butter. Add the sherry and simmer about 1 minute. Stir in the flour and cook another 2-3 minutes. Whisk in the milk, and add the onion juice, garlic, white pepper, and Worcestershire. Season with salt. Add the crabmeat and peppers, and cook slowly 20 minutes. Add the cream and cook until everything is warm. If desired, add nutmeg to provide a little spice to the soup. Transfer to individual serving bowls and garnish with parsley.

Yields 6 cups; serves 6

GREEN CHILE
SOUP FOR THE SOUL

*Both fresh and dried varieties of chiles have provided the
inspiration for soups and stews that can be enjoyed throughout the year. This
particular recipe combines the roasted flavor of poblanos with the bite of jalapeños. Both are never
better than at harvesttime, when their freshness and piquancy make a lively match with the cream
and cheese used in this recipe. Serve this soup with warm tortillas for a lunch
or opening course that will warm your heart as well as your soul.*

HEAT SCALE: *medium*
BEST USE: *fresh*

½ cup diced plum tomatoes
5 large poblano chiles, roasted,
   peeled, and seeded
1 jalapeño chile, seeded and
   quartered
3 tablespoons unsalted butter
1 small Vidalia onion, diced
3 tablespoons flour
2 cups chicken broth
1 cup heavy cream
4 ounces Monterey Jack cheese,
   shredded
¼ cup queso fresco, crumbled

In a blender or food processor,
process the tomatoes and chiles to
form a chunky purée. Set aside.

In a 2-quart or 4-quart stockpot,
heat the butter over medium heat.
Add the onions, cover the pot,
and sauté 5 minutes. Remove the
cover and add the flour. Cook
and stir over medium-low heat
2-3 minutes. Blend in the pepper
purée, then the chicken broth.
Bring the soup to a boil over
medium-high heat, stirring
continually to avoid sticking.
Reduce the heat to medium-low
and simmer partially covered
20-25 minutes.

Remove the soup from the heat
to allow it to cool and steep a bit.
Just before serving, return the soup
to a boil. Lower the heat to
medium-low, and blend in the
cream and Monterey Jack. (Be
sure to avoid too much heat under
the pot or the soup will curdle.)
Pour the soup into individual
serving bowls, sprinkle with
the queso fresco, and serve
immediately.

Yields 6-6½ cups; serves 4

*Note: This recipe can be easily
doubled and made a day in advance
when serving guests.*

RED BELL PEPPER SOUP

*The jalapeño chiles, tomatoes, garlic, lime, and cilantro add
a medley of volume and mirth to the stable yet mellow chicken broth
and potatoes. This recipe retains its richness and flavor when doubled, making
it a good choice for guests. If you like a little extra kick, garnish
each serving with a touch of freshly crushed red pepper.*

HEAT SCALE: **mild to medium**
BEST USE: **fresh**

4 cups chicken broth
2 jalapeño chiles, split lengthwise,
    deveined, and seeded
1 large red potato, peeled and
    chopped
4 plum tomatoes, seeded and
    diced
2 tablespoons olive oil
2 large cloves garlic, crushed
4 red bell peppers, seeded and
    chopped
salt and freshly ground black
    pepper, to taste
½ cup milk
½ cup heavy cream
zest and juice of 1 lime
1 cup sour cream, garnish
chopped fresh cilantro, garnish

Place the broth in a large sauce-pan. Add the chiles, potatoes, and tomatoes. Bring to a low boil over medium-high heat, then reduce the heat to medium-low. Simmer, covered, 20 minutes. Remove the chiles.

In a large frying pan, heat the oil over medium heat. Sauté the garlic and peppers 10-15 minutes, or until soft.

Combine the garlic and peppers with the broth, potatoes, and tomatoes in a blender. Process until smooth.

Return the mixture to the saucepan, and season with salt and pepper. Add the milk and cream, blending thoroughly. Reheat over low heat, so the soup does not boil. Add the lime zest and juice.

Transfer to individual serving bowls. Garnish with a spoonful of sour cream and cilantro.

Yields 7½-8 cups; serves 6

*top: Red Bell Pepper Soup (recipe this page);
bottom: Pizza with Peppers, Gjetost,
and Shrimp (recipe on page 104)*

SOUPS

117

HARVEST SOUP

The nutmeg, ginger, and bay leaf add a medley
of flavor and spice to the mellow peppers and pumpkin.
This soup needs little accompaniment, so I serve it with spice muffins
and a plate of sliced apples. This meal truly celebrates
the senses as well as the harvest.

HEAT SCALE: *mild*
BEST USE: *fresh*

4 tablespoons unsalted butter
1 large onion, chopped
3 scallions, green and white parts,
*   diced*
16 ounces canned pumpkin
1 yellow bell pepper, seeded
*   and chopped*
1 orange bell pepper, seeded
*   and chopped*
4 cups chicken broth
salt and freshly ground white
*   pepper, to taste*
½ teaspoon curry powder
large pinch of grated nutmeg
large pinch of ground ginger
1 bay leaf
1 cup heavy cream
chopped chives, garnish

In a large saucepan, melt the butter over medium heat. Sauté the onions and scallions 7 minutes, or until slightly golden. Add the pumpkin, peppers, broth, and spices. Bring the soup to a boil, reduce the heat, and simmer, uncovered, 15 minutes.

Take out the bay leaf, and purée all but 1 cup of the soup in a blender or food processor. Return the purée to the saucepan. Over medium heat, add the cream, stirring until the soup thickens. Transfer to individual serving bowls, and garnish with chives.

Yields 7½-8 cups; serves 6

TOMATO, ORANGE, AND PEPPER SOUP

*The tangy orange and tomato blend has proven to be more
compatible than many diners would imagine. This is not a rich soup,
yet it is full of flavor and very satisfying. The balance of ingredients makes it a soup
that can be consumed regularly without assaulting the taste buds. Freshly chopped
parsley adds color and spice. This soup also responds well to
a pinch of ground cloves. (Photo on page 88.)*

HEAT SCALE: **mild to medium**
BEST USE: **fresh**

2 small oranges, peeled and
   chopped
1 red bell pepper, roasted,
   peeled, seeded, and chopped
1 orange bell pepper, roasted,
   peeled, seeded, and chopped
12 fresh ripe tomatoes, peeled
   and chopped, or 12 canned
   tomatoes, drained and
   chopped
1 large clove garlic, chopped
2 tablespoons olive oil
2 tablespoons tomato paste
1½ cups chicken broth
3 tablespoons finely chopped
   fresh parsley
1 teaspoon sugar
salt and freshly ground black
   pepper, to taste
2 tablespoons cornstarch
4 tablespoons cold water

Blend the oranges in a food processor, leaving them slightly chunky. Set them aside.

Purée the peppers in a blender and set them aside.

In a soup pot, mix the tomatoes, garlic, oil, tomato paste, and broth. Add the pepper purée and bring to a boil, then lower the heat and partially cover the pot. Simmer gently 10-15 minutes. Stir in the parsley and sugar.

Season with salt and pepper. Add the oranges and stir to blend all of the ingredients.

In a small cup, mix the cornstarch and water to a smooth paste. Add an equal quantity of hot soup to the cornstarch, stir it well, and add it to the pot. Cook, stirring, until the soup comes to a boil and thickens, about 5-10 minutes. Simmer 2 minutes. Season with more salt and pepper, if desired. Serve immediately.

Yields 5½-7 cups; serves 4-6

MAIN DISHES

Paella (recipe on page 122)

PAELLA

*Valencia, Spain, is the heartland of paella. Many claim
this rice dish is more than a mark of culinary skill. To the residents
of that region, paella is a way of life, involving long discussions about the
authenticity of the ingredients used, as well as when and where it should be eaten. The paella
here was inspired by the information and opinions of many cooks over the years.
While experimentation has yielded many interesting results, this recipe is
the one that gets the most requests. (Photo on page 120.)*

HEAT SCALE: *mild*
BEST USE: *fresh*

1 pinch saffron threads
2 teaspoons sweet paprika
3 cups water
½ cup olive oil
6 jumbo shrimp, unpeeled
*one 3-pound chicken, skinned, cut
    into pieces, lightly floured, and
    dusted with salt and pepper*
*3 cloves garlic, peeled and finely
    chopped*
1 medium onion, chopped
*2 red or orange bell peppers,
    seeded and coarsely chopped*
*8 ounces fresh or bottled
    clam juice*
*2 cups paella rice or long-grain
    white rice*
*8 ounces fresh Italian flat green
    beans, slightly blanched, or
    one 10-ounce package frozen*
*12 mussels, scrubbed and
    removed of their beards*

In a heavy saucepan, toast the saffron over low heat about 1 minute. Remove it from the heat. When the saffron has cooled, add the paprika and water and set aside.

In a medium frying pan, heat half of the oil over medium-low heat. Add the shrimp and sauté 3-5 minutes, until slightly pink. Remove the shrimp and set aside.

In a paella pan or large frying pan, heat the remaining oil over medium-low heat. Sauté the chicken pieces until golden and almost cooked through. Remove the chicken and set aside.

Add the garlic, onions, and peppers to the paella pan and cook 3-5 minutes. Add the saffron mixture, clam juice, and rice and bring to a boil over medium-high heat. Reduce the heat to medium and cook, partly covered, 15 minutes, or until the rice is cooked and most of the liquid has been absorbed. Place the chicken, green beans, and mussels on top of the mixture, pressing each piece into the surface of the mixture. Cook another 10-15 minutes, until the mussels open and the rice swells a little more. Discard any unopened mussels. Add the shrimp on top of the mixture, and cook, partly covered, over low heat 5 minutes.

Remove the paella from the heat. Cover it with a kitchen towel and allow it to cool until warm, about 15 minutes.

Serves 6-8

Note: You can serve this dish on individual plates, or everyone can gather around the table and eat directly from the pan.

BIGOS
(HUNTER'S STEW)

*Uncle Joe is Italian, but his wife, Aunt Verna, is Polish. Our families
shared recipes and traditions not only during the holidays but also every day. I learned
a lot about Polish culture because of my aunt. The language is still beyond me, but a deep
appreciation of Polish tradition has remained with me since childhood. This recipe
is a variation of one of the oldest traditional Polish dishes. On colder
days this dish warms the body as well as the soul.*

HEAT SCALE: *mild*
BEST USE: *fresh or frozen*

*6 dried morels or fresh cremini
    mushrooms*
¼ cup water
2 pounds canned sauerkraut
*2 medium Granny Smith apples,
    peeled, cored, and chopped*
1 pound plum tomatoes, chopped
2 tablespoons tomato paste
*¼ teaspoon freshly ground
    black pepper*
2 red bell peppers, diced
1 bay leaf
*½ pound (2 cups) polish sausage,
    diced*
*¼ pound (1 cup) country sausage,
    diced*
6 slices bacon, coarsely chopped

Soak the dried mushrooms in
the water in a small bowl about
20 minutes, or until they have
plumped up to their near-original
size. Cut the reconstituted or fresh
mushrooms into quarters.

In a colander, rinse the sauerkraut and squeeze out all the
liquid. Place the sauerkraut in a
medium saucepan. Add the mushrooms and their liquid. Add the
apples, tomatoes, tomato paste,
black pepper, bell peppers, and bay
leaf. Cover and simmer over
medium-low heat 1¼ hours, or
until the broth has reduced and
thickened.

Add the sausages and bacon.
Cover and simmer 1 hour more.
Remove the stew from the heat
and allow it to cool. Transfer to a
storage container and refrigerate
2 days to let the flavors meld.
Remove the bay leaf and reheat
the stew to serve.

Yields 4-5 cups; serves 4-6

*Note: This stew freezes and reheats
well. I make a double batch of Bigos
and reserve half for the freezer.*

PENNE WITH PINE NUTS AND PEPPERS

Penne is a hollow tube of pasta, about 2 inches in length and 1⅖ inches in diameter. The surface is smooth, and the ends are diagonally cut. Smaller and lighter than mostaccioli, penne blends well with a variety of vegetables and sauces. Look for an imported dry variety made from durum wheat; its flavor and consistency will surpass that of domestic commercial products. ✍ *Lynn Rosetto Kasper in* The Splendid Table *shares a wealth of stories and folklore about pasta. She cites Piero Camporesi, a folklorist from the Emilio-Romagna region of Italy, as saying that many families celebrated the birth of a boy with penne. They celebrated the birth of a girl with lasagne.*

HEAT SCALE: *mild*
BEST USE: *fresh*

16 ounces penne
2 tablespoons olive oil
1 clove garlic, crushed
1 purple bell pepper, seeded, and
   sliced into ½-inch-wide strips
1 red bell pepper, roasted,
   peeled, seeded, and sliced
   into ½-inch-wide strips
4 plum tomatoes, seeded
   and chopped
2 tablespoons dry sherry
3 leaves opal basil, finely chopped
2 leaves lemon basil, finely
   chopped
1 fresh mint leaf, finely chopped
1 tablespoon balsamic vinegar
½-⅔ cup toasted pine nuts
salt and freshly ground black
   pepper, to taste

Cook the penne in a large pot of salted boiling water 12-15 minutes, or until *al dente*. Set aside in a colander to drain.

In a large frying pan, heat the oil over medium-low heat. Add the garlic and peppers and cook 10 minutes, or until the peppers become soft. Add the tomatoes, sherry, basil, mint, and vinegar, stirring to blend the flavors. Add the penne, cover, and cook over low heat 5 minutes. The penne should be warm but not hot. Remove the lid and add the pine nuts. Season with salt and pepper.

Serves 4

top: Penne with Pine Nuts and Peppers (recipe this page); bottom: Gnocchi (recipe on page 130)

POLENTA ON A BOARD

My first encounter with this particular recipe came when I was invited to a friend's house for Saturday night supper. Since polenta is one of my favorite dishes, I was prepared for a steamy, golden meal. I didn't expect to share my supper with the rest of his family whom I had never met, with all of us eating from the outer edges of the wooden board, working our way to the middle. While I was a bit timid at first, I picked up my fork and began to cut into my area, with what I hoped was a casual air of acceptance. Although I'm pretty sure that my hosts knew that their method of eating was new to me, my willingness to give it a go gained their approval. I was invited back to their house many times over the years, for many different meals, but that first supper with people I hardly knew taught me that mealtime has its own way of turning strangers into friends.

HEAT SCALE: *mild*
BEST USE: *fresh*

Topping
1 pound sweet Italian link
   sausage, cut into thirds, or bulk
   sausage, loosened with a fork
¼ cup olive oil
2 large cloves garlic, crushed
2 red bell peppers, seeded and
   chopped
2 green bell or yellow corno di
   toro peppers, seeded and
   chopped
1 Vidalia onion, chopped
½ teaspoon ground fennel seed
1 teaspoon dried oregano
½ teaspoon red pepper flakes

Polenta
3 cups boiling water
2 teaspoons salt
1 cup yellow cornmeal
shredded Parmigiano-Reggiano
   cheese, to taste

For the topping, place the sausage in a roasting pan or medium frying pan with ¼ inch of water. Loosely cover it with foil, and bake at 350°F or cook over medium heat 30 minutes. Drain and set aside.

Heat the oil a large frying pan over medium heat. Add the garlic and cook 2 minutes, or until tender and golden. Add the peppers and onions and cook uncovered over medium-low heat 20 minutes, or until soft. Add the fennel seed, oregano, and red pepper flakes. Toss the mixture and cook covered 5-7 minutes. Lower the heat to keep the mixture warm but not too hot.

For the polenta, bring the water to a boil in a small saucepan and add the salt. Slowly pour in the cornmeal. Stirring continuously, bring the mixture slowly to a boil. Lower the heat and simmer, stirring frequently, 20 minutes, or until the polenta is thick but not stiff.

Immediately pour the polenta onto a large, oiled wooden cutting board that will accommodate 4-6 people. Spread the polenta until it is ⅜ inch thick. Cover with the sausage and pepper topping. Top with the cheese.

Serves 6

Note: The sausage and pepper topping can be cooked a day ahead and set aside. Keep the sausage tightly wrapped, and remove it from the refrigerator about 1 hour before assembly. The pepper mixture actually tastes better if it is allowed to steep for a day. It too can be taken from the refrigerator about 1 hour before assembly time. When ready for final preparation, reheat the topping in a large frying pan. Once assembled, the polenta can be stored for a day or two in the refrigerator, but I prefer not to freeze this dish.

While this recipe is indeed fun to eat from a board, it can be arranged differently for a less intimate group. Pour the polenta onto a 10-inch or 12-inch oiled pizza pan. Spread the polenta into an 8-inch circle or square with a wet, metal spatula. Let stand 1 hour, then cover it and refrigerate until ready to use. When ready for assembly, warm the polenta 15 minutes in a 350°F oven. Cover the polenta with the topping and sprinkle with the cheese. Cut into slices and serve.

CHICKEN PAPRIKA

*Paprika is a pepper and a spice that creates a whole universe
of flavors, colors, and scents. I find that its addition to food creates a volume
of flavor that transforms veal, chicken, and stews into a magical treat. The Polish term
for chicken cooked with paprika is Kurcze w papryce. Traditional preparation calls for chicken,
onions, paprika, 1 tomato, half of a green bell pepper, and sour cream. This variation adds purple
bells for succulence and texture, and chiles for contrast to the mellow flavor of the
chicken and the smoothness of the sour cream. The result is a hearty, intense
main course that can be made a day ahead and warmed for guests.*

HEAT SCALE: *mild to medium*
BEST USE: *fresh*

*one 3-pound chicken, skinned and
    cut into pieces*
*1½ tablespoons Hungarian sweet
    paprika*
3 tablespoons butter
½ cup chopped onions
2 cloves garlic, minced
*1 purple bell pepper, roasted,
    peeled, seeded, and chopped*
*2 mild New Mexico chiles,
    roasted, peeled, seeded,
    and chopped*
*4 ounces cremini mushrooms,
    sliced*
1 teaspoon salt
*2 plum tomatoes, roasted,
    peeled, seeded, and chopped*
1 cup chicken broth
2 tablespoons tomato paste
3 tablespoons all-purpose flour
½ cup light cream or heavy cream
½ cup sour cream

Preheat the oven to 375°F.

Coat each piece of chicken with the paprika. Place the chicken in a baking dish and brown in the oven 12-15 minutes. Remove and set aside.

In a deep frying pan, melt the butter over medium heat. Sauté the onions and garlic until golden and slightly transparent. Add the peppers, chiles, mushrooms, salt, tomatoes, broth, and tomato paste. Cook, covered, over low heat 15 minutes. Add the chicken and cook, covered, 20 minutes. Uncover and cook 10 minutes longer. Remove the chicken from the pan, place it in the baking dish, cover, and keep it warm in the oven.

In a small bowl, whisk the flour and light cream until smooth. Pour it into the frying pan, stirring until blended and thickened. Return the chicken to the frying pan. Simmer 5 minutes over low heat, or until the mixture is heated through, spooning the liquid over the chicken. Remove from the heat and stir in the sour cream.

Serve with noodles or rice and baked apples, if you like.

Serves 4

Chicken Paprika (recipe this page)

MAIN DISHES

GNOCCHI

Kitchens in Germany, China, Ireland, and other countries issue one form of dumpling or another. The Piedmontese region of Italy came forth with gnocchi (little dumplings). ∿ *Gnocchi are frequently made from pumpkin, spinach blended with ricotta cheese, semolina, or potatoes. The people of Venice serve potato gnocchi with a simple marinara or mushroom sauce. This dish is treated like pasta and served as a second course. However, it's substantial enough for a main meal. I like to serve potato gnocchi with a salad of tossed greens, shaved Parmigiano-Reggiano cheese, tangerines, and apples. Gnocchi are also good with sour cream and freshly chopped chives and ham. A table cheese such as Asiago or Mizthritha makes a tangy accompaniment. (Photo on page 125.)*

HEAT SCALE: *medium*
BEST USE: *fresh or frozen*

1 pound russet potatoes
1 egg, slightly beaten
1 tablespoon dried and crushed
   mirasol chile
1 pinch of ground cinnamon
   or ground nutmeg
salt and freshly ground white
   pepper, to taste
½ cup sifted all-purpose flour

Scrub the potatoes. In a medium pot with plain water, boil the potatoes whole 30 minutes, or until cooked. Drain and set aside. Once the potatoes are cool enough to handle, peel them and put them in a medium bowl. Break them apart and mash them or put them through a ricer. Add the egg, chile, cinnamon or nutmeg, salt, and pepper. Stir with a fork and add half of the flour. Mix evenly. Add the remaining flour. Continue mixing the ingredients with your hands.

The dough will be sticky and smooth when ready for use. If necessary, add more flour, but in small amounts—too much will make the gnocchi tough.

Turn the dough onto a floured surface and cut it into 8 equal pieces. With floured hands, roll each piece into a rope about ½ inch to 1 inch in diameter and 8 inches to 9 inches long. (If the diameter is larger than 1 inch, the gnocchi may be too slow to cook, and if the diameter is less than ½ inch, the gnocchi tend to fall apart in boiling water.)

Using the tines of a fork or the arc on a pastry cutter, take a piece of dough about the size of a small walnut and roll it in the palm of your hand. You should have a conch-looking shape with ridges. Cut and roll the rest of the pieces.

Bring a large pot of salted water to boil. Once the bubbles appear on the surface, drop in the gnocchi in 3-4 batches, depending on the size of your pot. Be sure that the pot has a large enough bottom surface to accommodate all of the gnocchi, as they should fall to the bottom and form one layer. As they cook and become ready to serve, the gnocchi will rise to the surface of the water. Lift them out of the water with a slotted spoon and transfer them to a warm dish.

Serves 4

Note: Gnocchi freeze well and last in the freezer for about 2 months.

STUFFED CHICKEN BREAST

*This recipe calls for boneless chicken breasts, which
should be pink and firm, with little or no fat. Be sure to remove all
small particles of bone and any small pieces of fat or skin before preparation. This
main dish is fragrant and tender, enhanced by the chiles and herbs. If you want a
hotter chicken, use hot Hungarian chiles. This dish serves well
with sautéed mushrooms, corn, and zucchini.*

HEAT SCALE: *medium*
BEST USE: *fresh or frozen*

2 tablespoons butter
½ cup dry white wine
1 tablespoon dried oregano
2 cups chicken broth
6 boneless, skinless chicken
    breast halves, pounded to
    ⅜ inch thick
6 New Mexico Joe Parker or hot
    Hungarian chiles, roasted,
    peeled, seeded, and deveined
2 cups (8 ounces) shredded
    Monterey Jack or brick cheese
½ cup dry seasoned bread
    crumbs
minced fresh parsley, to taste

Preheat the oven to 350°F.

Melt the butter in a medium
saucepan over low heat. Add the
white wine and simmer 5 minutes.
Add the oregano and chicken
broth. Simmer another 5 minutes
and set aside.

Lay the chicken breasts on a
work surface. Place a chile on each
piece. Divide 1 cup of the cheese,
sprinkling some in the middle of
each breast at the shorter side and
rolling the chicken around it.
Coat each roll with the bread
crumbs. Pour the chicken broth
mixture into a large baking dish.
Place the chicken rolls in the dish,
seam side down. Sprinkle the
remaining cheese over the chicken
and bake 30 minutes. About
halfway through when the chicken
begins to turn golden, cover the
baking dish with a tent of foil to
keep the chicken from drying out.
Don't seal the edges, or the
chicken will stew instead of bake.
Add a little more water during
baking, if necessary. Sprinkle with
parsley before serving.

Serves 6

*Note: This dish can be frozen for
3-4 months. Roll the chicken around
the chiles and cheese, then put the rolls
in a container with the broth mixture
and freeze. When ready to eat, thaw
the rolls in the refrigerator, roll them in
the bread crumbs, and proceed with
the rest of the recipe. Use only fresh
chicken, not frozen and thawed,
if you're preparing this dish for
the freezer.*

FETTUCINE WITH SALMON AND PEPPER-LEMON CREAM SAUCE

*Lemons, limes, and other citrus fruits find themselves in perennial residence
in my kitchen. They are indispensable for salads, soups, poultry, fish, and a number of
baked goods. This blend of pasta, salmon, and pepper-lemon cream yields a satisfying yet light meal.
The toasted hazelnuts make this dish a special treat. ✎ Nearly all of the ingredients in this recipe
can be made a day in advance and then reheated for final preparation. This pasta dish
has good color and a slightly elegant look without appearing too formal.*

HEAT SCALE: *mild*
BEST USE: *fresh or frozen*

8 ounces salmon fillet
¼ cup dry sherry
¼ cup water
½ teaspoon dried dill
16 ounces egg fettucine
Pepper-Lemon Cream Sauce,
   1 recipe (see page 80)
4 ounces toasted hazelnuts,
   hulled
1 teaspoon chopped fresh
   tarragon or parsley or both

Place the salmon in a small frying pan with the sherry and water. Sprinkle the dill over the salmon. Cover and poach 6-7 minutes over medium heat. Remove from the stove, and allow the salmon to cool to room temperature. (If you are planning to use the salmon the following day, remove the skin, cover tightly, and refrigerate.)

Cook the fettucine in a large pot of salted boiling water 15-20 minutes, or until *al dente.*

While the pasta is cooking, separate the salmon into chunks and place them and any juices in a shallow saucepan. Add the Pepper-Lemon Cream Sauce, cover, and heat the entire mixture thoroughly but not to boiling over medium-low heat, 5 minutes. Lower the heat to warm.

Pour the pasta into a colander to drain, then transfer it to a heated bowl. Pour the cream and salmon over the fettucine. Add the hazelnuts and toss gently. Season with tarragon or parsley or both.

Serves 6

Note: This dish can be cooked and frozen for later use. When doing so, prepare as above, but cook the pasta just 7 minutes. Once this dish is thawed to room temperature, heat it 15-20 minutes in a 375°F oven.

PERFECT PASTA

Use the freshest pastas available, even if they are dry. Freshness is the key to the flavors and the colors of the meal.

Many people drown their pasta in sauce; rather they eat pasta with the sauce, not sauce with the pasta. Always use sauce and other ingredients to enhance, not cover the wonderful feel and taste of your noodles. Pasta and its accompaniments should form a lively yet balanced contrast on the taste buds.

I think that pasta is one of the most nurturing and healing foods one can eat. It doesn't need much embellishment in order to feed the body and the soul. Try it with a little olive oil, garlic, salt, and pepper.

Never overcook pasta. Fresh pasta takes 5–7 minutes to cook, while dry pasta can take 2–3 minutes longer. Of course, this all depends on what type of pasta is being cooked. Angel hair and capellini require less cooking time than rigatoni or tagliatelle, for instance.

Drain pasta just long enough to eliminate the excess cooking water. Never let it sit in the colander—unless, of course, you prefer to use it as a doorstop.

*Fettucine with Salmon and Pepper-Lemon
Cream Sauce (recipe this page)*

PEPPERONATA

This stew is very much like a Mediterranean ratatouille in character,
but it is easier to make and requires fewer assorted vegetables. It also reheats
better than ratatouille, as it holds its flavor and texture well. This dish is best served a day after
making it. ∽ I enjoy this recipe over rice or orzo, with a side of fresh mozzarella with
lemon zest. It's also good with a little grated Romano cheese and crusty garlic bread.
For a heartier dish, serve it with a basil-flavored pasta such as rotini or penne.

HEAT SCALE: *mild*
BEST USE: *fresh*

⅓ cup olive oil
1 orange bell pepper, roasted,
    peeled, seeded, and cut into
    ½-inch-wide strips
1 red bell pepper, roasted,
    peeled, seeded, and cut into
    ½-inch-wide strips
2 large onions, thinly sliced
2 cloves garlic, chopped
3 cloves elephant garlic, chopped
12 medium red tomatoes,
    skinned and chopped
one 12-ounce package of
    sun-dried red or yellow
    tomatoes, chopped
salt and freshly ground black
    pepper, to taste

In a large frying pan or deep
skillet, heat the oil over medium-
low heat. Add the peppers,
onions, and garlic. Sauté 15 minutes, or until the ingredients
soften and become slightly
translucent. Add the tomatoes.
Season with salt and pepper.
Simmer covered 30 minutes, then
set aside. Allow the pepperonata
to cool to room temperature, then
transfer to a storage container and
refrigerate overnight. Reheat,
partially covered, over medium
heat 15-20 minutes. Serve
immediately.

Yields 4 cups; serves 4

*Note: You may want to double or
triple the recipe and put some in
the freezer; I use doubled zip-top
freezer bags.*

PORK WITH PEPPERS, OLIVES, AND ROSEMARY

Rosemary is a pine-scented herb that has occupied gardens and kitchens for hundreds of years. It contains a wide range of medicinal properties as well as culinary advantages. This recipe combines rosemary with pork, but rosemary can also enhance soups, poultry, beef, fish, onions, and a number of vegetables and breads. Serve this dish with a side of pasta or long-grain and wild rice and warm applesauce.

HEAT SCALE: **mild**
BEST USE: **fresh or frozen**

one 4-pound boneless pork roast
6 tablespoons olive oil
6 cloves garlic, crushed and
   minced
⅓ cup roasted hazelnuts,
   chopped
1 tablespoon minced fresh
   rosemary
1 teaspoon chopped fresh sage
salt and freshly ground black
   pepper, to taste
1 medium onion, diced
1 cup dry Marsala wine
1 cup beef broth
1 red bell pepper, seeded and
   chopped
1 yellow bell pepper, seeded
   and chopped
½ cup cracked green olives
3 tablespoons minced fresh
   parsley

Put the roast on a cutting board. Cut along one long side to open it as much as possible without cutting all the way through. Rub the inside with 2 tablespoons of the oil. Generously spread the garlic, hazelnuts, rosemary, and sage in the inside. Roll the roast closed and tie it with string so that it doesn't open when cooking. Season with salt and pepper.

Preheat the oven to 350°F.

In a heavy, ovenproof frying pan that has been brushed with 2 tablespoons of the oil, gently brown the roast on all sides, about 15 minutes. Remove the roast from the pan, and cover loosely so that it retains most of its heat. Put the remaining oil in the pan and sauté the onions 5-7 minutes, or until golden. Push the onions to one side of the pan.

Return the roast to the pan. Place the onions over the roast, cover with a tent of foil, then put the pan in the oven. Roast 1½ hours, or about 20 minutes per pound. (If an ovenproof pan is not available, transfer the roast to a roasting pan before placing it in the oven.)

Place the wine in a large saucepan and bring it to a boil over medium-high heat. Lower the heat to low and simmer 5 minutes. Add the broth and cook another 5 minutes. Add the peppers, olives, and parsley. Cook, uncovered, 15 minutes, or until the liquid is reduced.

Spoon the pepper and olive mixture over and around the roast. Cover loosely with foil and roast another 20 minutes until the pork is cooked completely (160°F on a meat thermometer). Remove the pork from the oven and allow it to rest 15-20 minutes before slicing. Cut and remove the string from the roast.

Serves 8

Note: This dish freezes well. The pork can be sliced into ¾-inch pieces and placed in a freezer container. Top with the peppers and remaining juices and freeze. This keeps in the freezer for 3-4 months.

LINGUINE WITH VERY CHUNKY CLAM SAUCE

The addition of whole clams in their shells lends a touch of elegance to this dish. The combination of clams, peppers, and oregano offers flavor to egg, spinach, or tomato pasta. You can use linguine or experiment with fettucine or a light, delicate capellini. This recipe is also good using half egg linguine and half tomato fettucine. The different colors and widths of the pastas make for good visual contrast beneath the clams.

HEAT SCALE: *mild*
BEST USE: *fresh or frozen*

16 ounces egg linguine or tomato linguine
four 10-ounce cans whole baby clams
½ cup extra-virgin olive oil
4 tablespoons butter
½ cup chopped onions
6 cloves garlic, minced
1 teaspoon dried oregano
½ teaspoon fine sea salt
¼ teaspoon ground red pepper
½ cup minced fresh parsley
1 tablespoon fresh lemon zest
juice of ½ lemon
½-¾ cup roasted, peeled, and diced red bell peppers
12 small littleneck clams in the shell, steamed
freshly grated Parmigiano-Reggiano, to taste

Cook the linguine in a large pot of salted boiling water 12-15 minutes. Drain the clam juice from the canned clams, reserving 2 cups of the liquid. Set aside.

In a large frying pan, heat the oil and butter over medium heat. Sauté the onions and garlic 5 minutes, or until tender. Add the reserved clam juice, oregano, salt, and ground red pepper. Bring to a boil over high heat. Cook 3 minutes, then lower the heat to medium. Add the canned clams, parsley, lemon zest, lemon juice, and red bells. Cook 1 minute more.

Drain the linguine and transfer to a large serving bowl. Toss the clam sauce with the linguine. Add the steamed clams in the shell. Top with the cheese.

Serves 4-6

Note: When making a batch of this linguine for the freezer, cook the pasta 7 minutes; it will finish cooking when it's reheated.

top: Pepper and Tomato Salad (recipe on page 94); bottom: Linguine with Very Chunky Clam Sauce (recipe this page)

OTAK-OTAK

*Southeast Asia offers cuisine that combines a wide variety of subtle,
simple or complex, enticing dishes. This particular dish from Malaysia can be eaten
as soon as it's prepared or cooled and stored in the refrigerator to be eaten a day or two later.
There are many different custards of this kind, but this is my favorite. ᴖ The people of Malaysia
have historically cooked otak-otak by pouring the mixture into banana leaves and cooking them over hot coals.
Since banana leaves aren't readily available, an alternative method of oven steaming produces delicious
albeit not totally to origin results. This recipe also adapts well to wrapping the otak-otak in
individual foil packages that can be roasted on the grill. The result is a steamy,
savory confection that can be enjoyed with a salad and steamed corn.*

HEAT SCALE: **mild to medium**
BEST USE: **fresh**

2 pounds cod or orange roughy
1 teaspoon crushed dried ancho
   chile
10 Fresno chiles, seeded and
   deveined
1 large white onion
8 macadamia nuts
1 teaspoon ground ginger
6 cloves garlic
1 tablespoon turmeric
zest of ½ lemon
zest of ½ lime
3 eggs
2½ cups coconut milk
1 tablespoon sugar
salt, to taste

Cut the fish into small, flaky pieces and set aside. Process the chiles, onion, nuts, ginger, and garlic in a blender or food processor. Add the turmeric, lemon and lime zest and blend. Set aside.

Preheat the oven to 350°F.

Beat the eggs in a medium bowl. Add the coconut milk, fish, chile mixture, and sugar. Season with salt. Using a mixer, beat all of the ingredients 5-7 minutes, or until they are thoroughly mixed (the mixture will not be smooth).

Pour the mixture into a greased 3-quart baking dish. Bake 35-45 minutes, or until the mixture is set, just like a pudding. Turn off the oven and allow the pudding to rest 2-3 minutes before serving.

Yields 8 cups; serves 6

MONICA'S CHILAQUILES

*Tortillas play a vital role in Mexican life. Skillful hands and fertile
imaginations have utilized what the earth has offered to create tortillas from
flour, white corn, yellow corn, and blue corn. The tortillas are used fresh as well as slightly
stale, as in chilaquiles, which means broken-up, old sombreros. ✍ When preparing chilaquiles,
set the stale tortillas on baking sheets for about 8 hours, then cut them into strips. Don't let the tortillas
dry out too much before slicing them; they will crumble. But allow them to dry completely after
they're cut into strips. ✍ This recipe has been named for one shared with Monica,
my niece and a very talented cook. This recipe calls for blue-corn tortillas, but
yellow or white can be substituted. Using a combination of
blue and white makes a colorful dish.*

HEAT SCALE: *mild to medium*
BEST USE: *fresh*

4 cups water
2 cups chicken broth or bouillon
¼ cup brown sugar
2 teaspoons dried oregano
1 teaspoon anise seeds
*1 pound boneless, skinless
   chicken breast*
*1 dried ancho chile, seeded,
   deveined, and diced*
1½ cups sour cream
½ cup minced onions
2 cloves garlic, minced
*3 tablespoons finely chopped
   fresh cilantro*
2 cups vegetable oil
*12 blue-corn tortillas, cut into
   ¼-inch-wide strips*
*6 ounces grated cheddar
   cheese, Monterey Jack, or a
   combination of both*

Combine the water, broth, brown
sugar, oregano, and anise seeds in
a medium saucepan with a tight-
fitting lid. Bring the mixture to a
boil over medium heat. Lower the
heat and add the chicken. Cover
and simmer 15 minutes, or until
the chicken is cooked completely.
Cool the chicken and broth in the
refrigerator 15-20 minutes.
Remove the chicken and shred
it (the broth mixture can be
discarded). Mix the chicken with
the chiles in a medium bowl and
set aside.

In a small bowl, combine the
sour cream, onions, garlic, and
cilantro. Set aside.

Preheat the oven to 325°F.

In a large, deep saucepan, heat
the oil until it registers 365°F on a
cooking thermometer. Working in
batches, fry the tortilla strips until
crisp, about 1 minute. With a
slotted spoon, transfer them to
paper towels to drain.

In a large bowl, toss the chicken
mixture, tortilla strips, and cheese.
Spread evenly in a greased 3-quart
baking dish. Spoon the sour cream
mixture over the top and bake
25 minutes, or until heated
through. Serve with warm salsa or
tomatillo sauce.

Serves 4

GLACIER BASIN CHILI

*I have gone camping, taken hundreds of hikes, and enjoyed
a variety of picnics during my more than 20 years in Colorado. Escaping
to the mountains offers solitude and peace to otherwise hectic schedules. I developed
this practical dish for camping because a bowl of chili is very warming in the brisk mountain air,
but you don't have to go camping to enjoy it. The blend of beans and peppers receives
a crowning touch from the dried mirasol. This chili has a slight kick, and can be
enjoyed with your favorite cornbread and honey. If you like things
a little hotter, serve it with pickled jalapeños on the side.*

HEAT: **medium to hot**
BEST USE: **fresh or frozen**

1 pound black beans, rinsed,
  soaked, and well drained
1 dried mirasol chile, crushed
4 ounces bacon (6 slices)
1 small onion, finely chopped
1 purple bell pepper, seeded
  and chopped
2 serrano or jalapeño chiles,
  seeded, deveined, and diced
2 cloves garlic, minced
one 16-ounce can crushed
  tomatoes with juice
½-1 teaspoon ground epazote
½ teaspoon ground coriander
  seeds
salt, to taste

Place the beans and mirasols in a
large stockpot with water to
cover. Cook over medium heat
35 minutes, or until the beans are
nearly done. While the beans are
cooking, cook the bacon in a
frying pan over medium-low heat
10-15 minutes. Remove the
bacon, crumble it, and set it aside.
Sauté the onions, bell peppers,
serranos, and garlic in the bacon
drippings over medium-low heat
10 minutes, or just until the

peppers become slightly soft. Add
the vegetables and bacon to the
beans. Stir in the tomatoes,
epazote, and coriander. Cook
another 20 minutes, or until the
beans are very tender and the chili
has thickened. Season with salt.

Yields 8 cups; serves 4-6

*Note: For a heartier meal, add 1 cup
of diced pork to the pan of bacon,
onions, and peppers.*

*top: Pepper Corn Muffins (recipe on page 108);
bottom: Glacier Basin Chili (recipe this page)*

Lasagne with Meat Sauce and Four Cheeses

Lasagne, in many ways, is a rich yet restrained medley of flavors and texture.
This lasagne is tangy and substantial. My husband says that it weighs more than a newborn baby.
It probably does, since it contains pounds of cheese, meat, and sauce. However, a little goes a long way.
And this double-layer dish easily feeds a large group, especially when served with a salad of tossed mixed greens
and garlic bread. ∽ *The sauce easily adapts to recipes that call for no meat. In fact, the Pepper Lasagne recipe*
on pages 146-147 calls for meatless sauce. In each case, the sauce should be made a day in advance of
assembly. You can halve the sauce recipe for 12 servings or 6 cups of sauce. However, I like
to make the whole batch, using some fresh and freezing the rest. (Photo on page 145.)

HEAT: **mild**
BEST USE: **fresh or frozen**

Sauce
1 pound bulk Italian sausage
1½ pounds ground beef
1 pound lamb shank
1 teaspoon garlic powder
2 tablespoons olive oil
6 cloves garlic, sliced in half
two 28-ounce cans crushed
    tomatoes
two 12-ounce cans tomato paste
1 bay leaf
½ cup chopped fresh basil
1 sprig fresh rosemary
¼ cup chopped fresh thyme
1 cubanelle or corno di toro
    pepper, seeded and chopped
    coarsely
1 medium carrot, peeled and
    chopped
salt and freshly ground black
    pepper, to taste

Filling
two 24-ounce containers
    whole-milk ricotta cheese,
    at room temperature
2 eggs
½ cup chopped fresh parsley
¼ cup freshly grated Parmigiano-
    Reggiano cheese
¼ cup freshly grated Romano
    cheese
1 teaspoon ground white pepper
1 pinch freshly grated nutmeg

1½ pounds lasagne noodles with
    curly edges
two 8-ounce packages mozzarella
    cheese, shredded or sliced

For the sauce, preheat the oven to 350°F. Place the sausage and ground beef in a baking dish, keeping the meat loose and in small pieces. Brown the meat 20-30 minutes in the oven. Rub the lamb shank with the garlic powder and place it in a separate dish. Brown in the oven the same amount of time. Remove the meats from the oven, drain the fat from the pans, and pat the meats with paper towels. Set aside.

In a large stockpot, heat the oil over medium heat. Sauté the garlic until slightly golden. Add the tomatoes and 1 can of water for each can of tomatoes. Stir and blend. Add the tomato paste and 2 cans of water for each can of paste. Blend thoroughly with a whisk or slotted spoon. Add the bay leaf, basil, rosemary, thyme, peppers, and carrots. Season with salt and pepper and blend.

Cook the mixture over medium heat, making sure that it doesn't stick. When the sauce is bubbly, add the meats, leaving the lamb shank whole. Simmer over medium-low heat 2 hours, or until the liquid is reduced by 1½ inches to 2 inches.

Once the sauce has reached the desired thickness, remove it from the heat. Remove the bay leaf and lamb shank. Refrigerate the lamb to be eaten separately another time or cut it up and return it to the sauce. Refrigerate the sauce overnight.

The next day, season the sauce with more basil and salt and reheat over low heat.

For the filling, use a mixer at medium-low speed to stir the ricotta in a large bowl. Add the eggs one at a time and blend. Add the parsley, Parmigiano-Reggiano, Romano, white pepper, and nutmeg, blending them into the mixture. Set aside.

Preheat the oven to 375°F. In a roasting pan with boiling salt water, cook the lasagne 3 or 4 noodles at a time 6-7 minutes. The noodles should be pliable but not soft. With tongs, place the noodles between sheets of waxed paper.

To assemble, pour 1 cup of the sauce into a lasagne baking dish to just cover the bottom. Lay 3 or 4 strips of noodles, depending upon the width of your pan, on top of the sauce. Gently spoon half of the ricotta filling over the noodles. Place one-third of the mozzarella slices on top of the filling. Spoon 1½ cups of the sauce

over the mozzarella. Put down another layer of noodles, then the remaining filling, one-third of the mozzarella, and 1½ cups sauce. Top with a layer of noodles, 2 cups sauce, and the remaining mozzarella.

Bake uncovered 40-45 minutes, or until the cheese and sauce are bubbly. Turn off the oven, and cover the lasagne with foil. Seal the sides of the dish with foil, but puncture the top of the foil with a fork to allow steam to escape. Let the lasagne set 15 minutes in the oven. Serve the lasagne warm when it's firm to the touch; if you cut the lasagne while it's hot, it will be watery.

Serves 24

Note: The sauce keeps well 3-4 months in the freezer.

CHICKEN CACCIATORE

*While the chicken for this dish tastes best
when cooked just before serving, the sauce can be made
in advance and frozen. When doing so, reduce the cooking time to
20 minutes; the sauce will finish cooking when combined with the chicken and
baked in the oven. This recipe also doubles easily, with adjustments to the
herbs and spice to taste. The sauce tastes best when made a day
in advance and spooned onto the chicken at baking time.*

HEAT SCALE: *mild*
BEST USE: *fresh*

*2 purple bell peppers, seeded
    and cut into ½-inch-wide strips*
*2 red bell peppers, seeded and
    cut into ½-inch-wide strips*
*2 yellow bell peppers, seeded and
    cut into ½-inch-wide strips*
*1 large onion, cut into ¼-inch-
    wide slices*
4 cloves garlic, minced
1 tablespoon dried oregano
*salt and freshly ground black
    pepper, to taste*
*two 28-ounce cans crushed plum
    tomatoes*
one 3-inch sprig fresh rosemary
¼ cup fresh lemon thyme
1 bay leaf
28 ounces water
1 pound mushrooms, sliced
*two 1-1½-pound chickens,
    skinned and cut into pieces*
¼ cup extra-virgin olive oil
2 cups flour

Set the peppers and onions in a large bowl and toss with the garlic and oregano. Season with salt and pepper. Let stand 10 minutes.

In a large stockpot, combine the tomatoes, rosemary, thyme, and bay leaf. Add the water and lightly season with more salt and pepper. Cook over medium heat 10-20 minutes, or until the sauce bubbles. Add the pepper mixture and mushrooms. Cook 30 minutes, stirring to prevent the sauce from sticking. If it begins to boil, lower the heat. Remove from the heat and let it cool about 2 hours. Cover the sauce and transfer it to the refrigerator overnight.

Preheat the oven to 350°F.

Place the chicken in a large, deep roaster. Brush each piece with a little oil, then dust with the flour. Bake 30 minutes. Add the sauce. Bake, lightly covered with foil, 1 hour, basting the chicken every 20 minutes.

Serves 10-12

Note: If the sauce is frozen, thaw it and heat it to simmering before adding it to the chicken.

*top: Chicken Cacciatore (recipe this page);
center: Lasagne with Meat Sauce and
Four Cheeses (recipe on pages 142-143);
bottom: Pepper Lasagne (recipe on pages 146-147)*

PEPPER LASAGNE

*This recipe calls for most of the ingredients required
for the Lasagne with Meat Sauce and Four Cheeses (see pages 142-143)
with some variations. This dish's additional layers of green peppers and opal basil,
then yellow peppers and opal basil make for a colorful presentation
when topped with the deep red sauce. (Photo on page 145.)*

HEAT: **mild**
BEST USE: **fresh or frozen**

Sauce
2 tablespoons olive oil
6 cloves garlic, sliced in half
two 28-ounce cans crushed
    tomatoes
two 12-ounce cans tomato paste
1 bay leaf
2 tablespoons fresh minced
    oregano
½ cup chopped fresh basil
1 sprig fresh rosemary
¼ cup chopped fresh thyme
1 cubanelle or corno di toro
    pepper, seeded and chopped
    coarsely
1 medium carrot, peeled and
    chopped
salt and freshly ground black
    pepper, to taste

Filling
two 24-ounce containers
    whole-milk ricotta cheese,
    at room temperature
2 eggs
½ cup chopped fresh parsley
¼ cup freshly grated Parmigiano-
    Reggiano cheese
¼ cup freshly grated Romano
    cheese
1 teaspoon ground white pepper
1 pinch freshly grated nutmeg

1½ pounds lasagne noodles with
    curly edges
2 cubanelle or corno di toro
    peppers, peeled, seeded,
    sliced, and squeezed of excess
    water
two 8-ounce packages mozzarella
    cheese, shredded or sliced
¼ cup finely chopped fresh
    opal basil
2 yellow bell peppers, peeled,
    seeded, sliced, and squeezed of
    excess water

For the sauce, heat the oil over medium heat in a large stockpot. Sauté the garlic until slightly golden. Add the tomatoes and 1 can of water for each can of tomatoes. Stir and blend. Add the tomato paste and 2 cans of water for each can of paste. Blend thoroughly with a whisk or slotted spoon. Add the bay leaf, oregano, basil, rosemary, thyme, peppers, and carrots. Season with salt and pepper and blend.

Cook the mixture over medium heat, making sure that it doesn't stick. When the sauce is bubbly, lower the heat to medium-low and simmer 2 hours, or until the liquid is reduced by 1½ inches to 2 inches.

Once the sauce has reached the desired thickness, remove it from the heat. Remove the bay leaf, and refrigerate the sauce overnight. The next day, season the sauce with more basil and salt and reheat over low heat.

For the filling, use a mixer at medium-low speed to stir the ricotta in a large bowl. Add the eggs one at a time and blend. Add the parsley, Parmigiano-Reggiano, Romano, white pepper, and nutmeg, blending them into the mixture. Set aside.

Preheat the oven to 375°F. In a roasting pan with boiling salt water, cook the lasagne 3 or 4 noodles at a time 6-7 minutes. The noodles should be pliable but not soft. With tongs, place the noodles between sheets of waxed paper.

To assemble, pour 1 cup of the sauce into a lasagne baking dish to just cover the bottom. Lay 3 or 4 strips of noodles, depending upon the width of your pan, on top of the sauce. Gently spoon half of the ricotta filling over the noodles. Place the cubanelle peppers over the filling, then half of the basil. Cover the basil with one-third of the mozzarella slices. Spoon 1½ cups of the sauce over the mozzarella. Put down another layer of noodles, then the remaining filling, the yellow peppers, the remaining basil, one-third of the mozzarella, and 1½ cups sauce. Top with a layer of noodles, 2 cups sauce, and the remaining mozzarella.

Bake uncovered 40-45 minutes, or until the cheese and sauce are bubbly. Turn off the oven, and cover the lasagne with foil. Seal the sides of the dish with foil, but puncture the top of the foil with a fork to allow steam to escape. Let the lasagne set 15 minutes in the oven. Serve the lasagne warm when it's firm to the touch; if you cut the lasagne while it's hot, it will be watery.

Serves 24

Note: I also like this lasagne with chopped portobello or porcini mushrooms added as another layer on top of the peppers. Use 1 cup mushrooms per layer.

STUFFED PEPPERS

Harvest time meant a kitchen lined with pans of stuffed peppers
when I was growing up. As with many foods, we ate the most of what became
available as the suns of August and September began to issue a reward for weeks of cultivation
and nurturing. Stuffed peppers require plenty of sauce for moisture and should not be tightly packed with
stuffing. Since the filling expands during the baking process, too much disallows moisture from getting
into the ingredients. The result will be a dry, chewy, pretty tasteless mix. The recommendation
for the meatball is the same as for the stuffed pepper: keep it loose.

HEAT SCALE: *mild*
BEST USE: *fresh*

6-8 green, red, or yellow
    bell peppers
⅔-1 pound ground beef
⅔-1 pound ground pork
⅔-1 pound ground lamb
½ cup uncooked long-grain rice
1 medium onion, minced
1 cup minced parsley
2 cloves garlic, crushed
½ cup freshly grated Romano
    cheese
2 teaspoons salt
freshly ground black pepper,
    to taste
1 pinch dried mint
two 12-ounce cans tomato paste
24 ounces water

Preheat the oven to 350°F.

Cut a slice from the top of each pepper and remove the seeds and membranes. Blanch the green peppers 3 minutes in boiling water. (There's no need to blanch red or yellow peppers.) Set aside.

Mix the meats (use the smaller amount if the peppers are not large), rice, onions, parsley, garlic, cheese, salt, and pepper in a large bowl, making sure that the meat is broken up. Sprinkle the mint over the mixture and blend gently with a fork without overworking the meat. Stuff the peppers loosely. Place the peppers in a baking pan that is at least 2 inches higher than the peppers. (You'll need to baste them while they bake, and will need room to make sure that everything is covered.)

In another large bowl, whisk the tomato paste and water. Using a measuring cup or ladle, pour the tomato mixture over each pepper, making sure that 1 inch of the liquid is in the bottom of the pan when finished. Cover the peppers tightly with a piece of foil, and bake 1 hour, basting the peppers every 15-20 minutes. When the rice is tender, remove the peppers from the oven. Let stand 5-7 minutes before serving.

Yields 6-8

Indios Vestidos
(recipe on page 150)

INDIOS VESTIDOS

This spicy but not too hot dish, which is whimsically named "Dressed Indians" or
"Little Indians," is an adaptation of one I found years ago in Diana Kennedy's The Tortilla Book.
It's delicious with homemade sour cream, the recipe for which follows this one. ✍ *I made Indios Vestidos*
for the first time in 1982 at a family gathering. I proceeded to make the enchiladas, as my father hovered over
the skillet. He had appointed himself the official taste tester or, in his mind, the sacrificial lamb of the family. I
placed an enchilada on his plate, adding sauce, table cheese, and homemade sour cream on the side. He took one
bite without sour cream, then one with, then another without. I thought he was going to lick the plate. But,
instead, he looked at me solemnly and said, "You can get married now." Then he winked, pinched my
cheek, and gave me a big smile. I'm glad he sanctioned my suitability as a wife because by
that time I had been married for five years. (Photo on page 149.)

HEAT SCALE: *medium*
BEST USE: *fresh*

Filling
5 black peppercorns
1 tablespoon coarse sea salt
2 cloves garlic, peeled
1 small onion, chopped
1 pound boneless pork roast or
    tenderloin
1 poblano chile, roasted, peeled,
    seeded, and chopped
1 golden bell pepper, seeded and
    chopped
1 dash ground cinnamon

Sauce
2½ pounds broiled tomatoes,
    or 4 cups canned chopped
    tomatoes
2 tablespoons peanut oil
½ medium onion, finely chopped
8 ounces tomato paste
8 ounces water
1 canned chipotle chile, diced
1 fresh jalapeño chile, diced
½ teaspoon salt
juice of ½ lime

twelve 6-inch flour tortillas
4 large eggs, separated
½ teaspoon salt
1½ cups flour
⅓ cup peanut oil
1 large avocado, sliced and
    drizzled with lime juice,
    optional
crumbled dry queso fresco,
    to taste
Sour Cream, 1 recipe (see
    page 151)

For the filling, place the pepper-corns, salt, garlic, onions, and pork in a medium saucepan and add just enough water to cover everything. Bring the mixture to a boil over medium-high heat, then lower. Cover and simmer 45 minutes, or until the pork is tender.

Remove the mixture from the heat and set aside to cool. Once the pork can be handled, take it out of the saucepan and shred it (the rest of the mixture can be discarded). Combine the pork with the chiles, bell peppers, and cinnamon in the saucepan. Cover and keep the pork warm, or refrigerate it for future use.

For the sauce, preheat the broiler if using fresh tomatoes. Place the fresh tomatoes in a shallow pan or on a baking sheet. Broil them 6 inches from the heat source, turning them from side to side. Cook 20-25 minutes, or until the tomato skins are blistered and brown but not black. Allow the tomatoes to cool, then chop them.

Heat the oil in a large frying pan over medium heat. Sauté the onions until soft. Add the tomatoes, tomato paste, water, chiles, salt, and lime juice. Whisk the ingredients, making sure that the tomato paste has completely blended with the other ingredients. Cook 30 minutes and set aside.

To assemble, place about ¼ cup of the filling onto the tortillas. Roll the tortillas closed, and place them seam side down on a large baking sheet or pan. Set aside.

In a medium bowl, beat the egg whites and salt until stiff. Add the egg yolks and beat until they are blended into the mixture. Dip the rolled tortillas into the flour and then into the egg mixture to lightly coat. Place the tortillas in a large frying pan with the oil, and cook until golden brown. Transfer the tortillas to paper towels to drain and then onto a serving platter. Cover with the sauce and garnish with the avocado slices, if

desired. Top with the queso fresco and sour cream and serve at once. (The enchiladas can remain on a baking sheet in a 350°F oven about 10-15 minutes. After that, they lose their crunch.)

Yields 12

Note: The pork filling can be prepared 2-3 days in advance, allowing for quicker and easier preparation.

SOUR CREAM
1 cup whipping cream
2 tablespoons buttermilk

Place the cream and buttermilk in a 1-quart glass canning jar, screw on the lid, and shake a few seconds until the ingredients are well mixed. Take the lid off of the jar, and set the jar near a pilot light or warm spot on the stove to thicken. Be sure the spot is not too warm, otherwise the mixture will form a skin on top and the cream will taste cooked. Let stand 6-8 hours, until the mixture has the consistency of a milkshake.

Gently move the jar from the stove to the refrigerator. Allow the mixture to thicken another 8 hours before serving.

Yields 1½ cups

Note: This amount of sour cream is what you will need for this dish. Be sure to make only the amount you need because unlike commercial sour cream, it contains no stabilizers or preservatives, so it doesn't store well.

CONDIMENTS

FAVORITE
MADRAS CURRY

*This is a variation of madras curry, known by many
to be the "all-purpose" curry blend. This mix has a pungent, slightly
sweet aroma and blends well with milder meats and vegetables. I like to add it
to jasmine rice cooked in equal amounts of coconut milk and chicken broth.
This blend calls for dried cilantro, but finely chopped fresh cilantro
can be used if you're preparing this mix for immediate use.*

HEAT SCALE: *medium*
BEST USE: *fresh*

4 tablespoons ground dried
   New Mexico ancho chile
2 teaspoons ground dried mirasol
   chile
3 tablespoons ground coriander
   seeds
4 tablespoons ground cumin
   seeds
1 teaspoon ground ginger
1 teaspoon ground fennel seeds
1 tablespoon ground cardamom
1 tablespoon ground cloves
1 teaspoon crushed dried cilantro

Mix all the ingredients in a small
bowl with a fork or whisk. Use
immediately or store in an air-
tight pint jar or plastic container.

Yields 1 cup

*Note: This mix can be made in
batches and stored in the pantry
3-6 months.*

CHILE NUT MIX

*The origin of this nut mix began when I tasted my first
chile-coated pistachios. Since then I have experimented with a variety
of nut and pepper combinations. You can regulate the heat of this dish by adjusting
the use of the pepper. This recipe calls for dried mirasol, which has a lovely aroma and
a rather low-key yet penetrating heat. If you're experimenting with pepper-nut combinations,
make a batch of the mix and let it sit for a day before tasting to determine whether or
not to increase the quantity of chile to attain the heat you desire. The nuts
can be easily made the day you are expecting guests or stored in an
air-tight container in a cool, dry place for several weeks.*

HEAT SCALE: **hot**
BEST USE: **fresh**

8 ounces raw peanuts, shelled
8 ounces raw pecan halves
8 ounces raw almonds
8 ounces raw pistachios,
   unshelled
¼ cup peanut oil
1 tablespoon garlic powder
½ teaspoon red pepper flakes
½ teaspoon paprika
½ teaspoon crushed dried
   mirasol or ancho chile
½ teaspoon dried cumin
1 tablespoon fine sea salt
1 tablespoon fresh lime juice

Place the nuts on a rimmed baking
sheet and refrigerate at least
1 hour.

Preheat the oven to 375°F. In a
large bowl, combine the oil,
spices, and lime juice. Blend
thoroughly with a whisk. Add the
nuts, stirring to coat them well.
Place the nuts in a large cast-iron
skillet or on a baking sheet. Bake
7-12 minutes, or until the nuts are
toasty. Allow the nuts to cool
until they are slightly warm,
then serve.

Yields 8 cups

HOT HUNGARIANS WITH GARLIC AND MINT

As with the handling of many chile varieties,
the use of rubber gloves is essential for the hot Hungarian
wax chile. The use of mint adds a little relief to this very hot, pervasive
condiment. I have used lemon mint, apple mint, and peppermint
with the peppers and garlic. All add a special flavor.

HEAT SCALE: *hot*
BEST USE: *canned*

1½ cups distilled vinegar
½ cup white wine vinegar
5-8 hot Hungarian wax chiles,
    pierced
3 cloves garlic
6 leaves apple or lemon mint,
    or a mix of both
½ teaspoon fine sea salt

In a small, enamel saucepan, bring the vinegars to a gentle boil. Reduce the heat to low.

Cut the stems from the peppers and set aside. (The peppers will be packed whole.)

Place the garlic, mint, and salt in a hot, sterilized quart jar. Pack the peppers, tapered end first, filling the jar as tightly as possible without bruising the peppers. Cover with the vinegar, leaving ¼-inch headspace. Screw the lid and ring tightly on the jar, and process 12 minutes in a boiling-water bath. Remove the jar from the water and let stand in a draft-free area until the lid has popped.

Yields 1 quart

Note: These canned peppers keep well 6-10 months. Refrigerate after opening.

PAPRIKA

Paprika peppers contain light, longitudinal ridges that carry the seeds. If you desire a mellow but still flavorful powder, don't include the ridges or the seeds when grinding. However, if it's a coarser, tangier product you prefer, grind the ridges and seeds along with the rest of the pepper.

When using paprika in recipes, don't allow it to heat for too long in oil; it loses color and flavor. Rather, brown your meats or vegetables and then sprinkle or rub paprika onto them. Allow the meats or vegetables to sit about 5 minutes, then continue cooking.

Mild paprikas are brighter and more colorful than their darker, hotter cousins. If you want to add color to a dish, select a mild paprika. If you're trying to achieve a stronger flavor and heat, use a darker pepper. Sweet Hungarian paprika adds zest to grains, soups, stews, poultry, and a variety of casseroles.

Although Hungary is now considered by many to be the country of origin for paprika, the pods probably came to Hungary as a result of Turkish influence. The Hungarians followed the Turkish tradition of harvesting, drying, and crushing the red pods into a fine powder that was used to season various dishes.

According to Hungarian legend, a high-ranking citizen or *pasha* named Mehmet lived a privileged life in Budapest during the 1600s. A pretty watergirl caught Mehmet's eye one day. He was so enchanted by her that he brought her into his harem.

The watergirl spent most of her days wandering through the colorful pathways of Mehmet's walled garden. In addition to ornamental plants and flowers, the garden housed edible pods that grew on strange, meandering vines.

The *pasha* and his harem ate the red pepper regularly, and the watergirl came to delight in the flavor and aroma. She began secretly collecting the seeds, planning one day to create a garden of her own.

The watergirl dreamed of her future and the young man from whom she was taken but still loved. Finally, she found a secret passage from the palace to the countryside, an escape route Mehmet devised in case he ever needed to flee the palace. Eventually, the watergirl met her lover every evening without being noticed. She gave her lover a bag of the red pepper seeds and instructed him to sow them.

The young man obeyed, and after some months, the winding vines of the pepper plant charmed their way

around Budapest. Citizens from all parts of the city tried the spice and loved the flavor and aroma it added to foods. The red pepper became something of an obsession and remained so throughout the course of revolutions and invasions that pervaded Europe. The paprika traveled from country to country, growing in abundance, perhaps casting a lover's spell over all who tasted it.

If you want to cultivate a row or two of the peppers in your garden and you live in a long growing-season area, allow the peppers to dry on the plants. In shorter growing-season areas, these peppers can be purchased or picked when mature and hung in a well-ventilated spot to dry. These peppers can also be dried in a 150°F oven, but the results aren't always reliable because the peppers can toast and become too dark. To dry them in the oven, poke a small hole in each pepper so moisture can escape. Arrange the peppers on baking sheets or in shallow baking pans and place them in the oven 8-10 hours, or until dry.

The peppers can be coarsely ground in a food processor or finely ground with a mortar and pestle or coffee mill. Dried peppers can also be stored whole in a cool, dry pantry or in the freezer, then ground fresh for each recipe.

PAN-ROASTED RED BELL PEPPERS

*Roasted peppers are so easy to prepare that I add them
to a meal almost as an afterthought during the fall, when peppers are abundant.
I particularly enjoy roasting red bells along with orange and yellow ones. I arrange them on a platter
and garnish them with basil, garlic slices, and extra-virgin olive oil. They are even easier to eat
than they are to roast. Enjoy these peppers frequently but in moderation
if you don't want to smell like peppers and garlic!*

HEAT SCALE: *mild*
BEST USE: *canned*

⅓ cup extra-virgin olive oil
6 large red bell peppers
¾ cup water
¾ cup distilled vinegar
4 cloves garlic, peeled and sliced
2 tablespoons chopped curly
   opal basil
1 teaspoon fine sea salt

In a large frying pan, heat the oil over medium heat. Sauté the peppers whole and with their stems, turning frequently with tongs until all sides begin to turn a slight toasty brown, about 20 minutes. The skin will begin to bubble and swell, but the flesh will remain firm. Remove the peppers from the pan and set them aside until they are cool enough to handle.

Combine the water and vinegar in a small saucepan, and bring to a gentle boil over medium heat.

In each of 2 hot, sterilized pint jars, place 2 cloves garlic, 1 tablespoon basil, and ½ teaspoon salt. Remove the stems and skins from the peppers. Slit one side and lay the peppers flat to clean the insides, using a grapefruit spoon or fork to remove the seeds. Roll up the peppers, and pack them into the jars. Cover with the vinegar mixture, leaving ¼-inch headspace. Screw the lids and rings tightly on the jars, and process 10-12 minutes in a boiling-water bath. Remove the jars from the water and let stand in a draft-free area until the lids have popped. Allow the peppers to stand 2 weeks before consuming.

Yields 2 pints

Note: These peppers can be eaten as a side dish with a little more olive oil, salt, and black pepper added at serving time. They can also be added to pasta or various hot dishes calling for roasted peppers. This dish is good with slices of mozzarella garnished with salt, black pepper, and lemon juice. Add a loaf of bread and a plate of sliced ham, and lunch is ready.

RASPBERRY, GOLDEN RAISIN, JALAPEÑO JAM

*Red raspberries combine with the heat of
the jalapeño to create a flavor that enhances bread as well
as rice. You'll need to experiment with applications
and find your own favorites.*

HEAT SCALE: **mild to medium**
BEST USE: **canned**

2½ cups frozen unsweetened
   raspberries, crushed
2 cups golden raisins
1 cup sugar
1 cup seeded and chopped
   jalapeño chiles

Put the frozen raspberries, raisins, and sugar in a frying pan. Cook over medium-high heat, bringing the mixture to a boil. Turn down the heat and, stirring continuously, cook 20-30 minutes, or until the mixture is thick and clings to the spoon. Add the chiles, blending them into the mixture, and cook another 20 minutes, or until bubbly.

Pour the mixture into hot, sterilized half-pint jars, leaving ¼-inch headspace. Screw the lids and rings tightly on the jars, and process 15 minutes in a boiling-water bath. Remove the jars from the water and let stand in a draft-free area until the lids have popped.

Yields 4 half-pints

PICKLED JALAPEÑOS

*I like to make pickled jalapeños with generous amounts of garlic
and basil. I've used opal basil, as well as the green Genovese, variegated opal/green,
and lemon basil. Each lends a distinct personality to the jalapeños. Be sure to pierce the
jalapeños slightly for canning. This allows the liquid and, consequently,
the scents and flavors to pervade the flesh of these capsicums.*

HEAT SCALE: *hot*
BEST USE: *canned*

3 pounds jalapeño chiles
salt, to taste
12 large cloves garlic
18 leaves opal basil
12 leaves lemon mint
12 small sprigs oregano
3 bay leaves, halved
6-8 cups distilled vinegar,
  boiling hot

Rinse and pierce the chiles once with a fork. In each of 6 hot, sterilized pint jars, put some salt, 2 cloves garlic, 3 basil leaves, 2 mint leaves, 2 sprigs oregano, and ½ bay leaf. Cut the stems from the chiles, then pack them into the jars, with the tapered end going in first. Pack as tightly as possible without bruising the flesh of the chiles. Cover with the vinegar, leaving ¼-inch headspace. Screw the lids and rings tightly on the jars, and process 10-12 minutes in a boiling-water bath. Do not overprocess, as this will cause the peppers to lose color dramatically. Remove the jars from the water and let stand in a draft-free area until the lids have popped. These chiles should stand 2-3 weeks before consuming. Refrigerate after opening.

Yields 6 pints

Very Veracruz Mayonnaise

The chipotle is a smoked chile pepper, frequently the jalapeño, while the chipotle in adobo is the smoked chile that has been combined with a tangy paste made from herbs, ground chile, and vinegar. This chipotle mayonnaise offers a creamy, spicy volume to raw bell pepper strips, celery, hard-boiled egg halves, and chilled shellfish. It is also perfect for basting grilled bluefish, tuna, or swordfish. This recipe calls for either dried or canned chipotles. Canned chipotles don't need to be reconstituted before use, but dried ones do. Sauté dried chipotles whole in a little olive oil, then set aside in a small bowl to cool 5 minutes. Add 1½ cups water and allow the peppers to soak 10-15 minutes before using.

HEAT SCALE: **hot**
BEST USE: **fresh**

2 cloves garlic, crushed
¼ cup fresh lime juice
3 egg yolks
1¼ cups olive oil
3 dried or canned chipotles
   in adobo
1 teaspoon fine sea salt
chopped fresh cilantro, to taste

In a blender, purée the garlic and lime juice. Blend in the egg yolks. With the motor running, slowly drizzle the oil into the mixture, allowing it to be completely absorbed. Add the chipotles and salt, and blend another 30 seconds. Pour into a storage container. When serving, season with cilantro.

Yields 1-1½ cups

Note: This condiment keeps well in the refrigerator for up to 1 week.

ORANGE-PEPPER MARMALADE

*This marmalade can be thick or thin, depending upon
your intended use. When it's thin, it can be used to baste ribs
or chicken for the grill, and it adds volume to rice and black beans. I make
both consistencies and use the thicker of the two for biscuits, corn muffins, homemade
zucchini bread, and whole-grain toast. Thicken the sauce by reducing the
amount of water used and by allowing the mixture to sit uncovered
until the liquid has evaporated by about ¼ inch.*

HEAT SCALE: *medium*
BEST USE: *canned*

3 cups water
4 oranges, peeled, seeded,
   and chopped
½ lime, thinly sliced
3 cups puréed but still slightly
   chunky fresh pineapple
4½ cups sugar
½ cup chopped or slivered
   blanched almonds
6 jalapeño chiles, seeded
   and diced

Combine the water, oranges, and lime slices in a medium saucepan. Cook, covered, over medium-high heat 30 minutes. Remove from the heat and let stand overnight in a cool place.

Add the pineapples to the pan with the orange mixture and simmer over medium heat 15 minutes. Add the sugar, 1 cup at a time, stirring until the sugar dissolves. Increase the heat to high. Boil the mixture, stirring frequently, until it thickens and registers 220°F on a candy thermometer. Blend in the almonds and chiles.

Pour the mixture into hot, sterilized half-pint jars, leaving ¼-inch headspace. Screw the lids and rings tightly on the jars, and process 10-12 minutes in a boiling-water bath. Remove the jars from the water and let stand in a draft-free area until the lids have popped.

Yields 4 half-pints

ITALIAN PEPPERS IN GARLIC, LEMON, AND OLIVE OIL

*Lemon adds a light and tangy flavor to this garlic,
pepper, olive oil trio. These peppers can be prepared for the pantry
and stored 6-8 months. Or serve them fresh with bread and a salad of red, orange,
and yellow tomatoes garnished with celery, lemon thyme, a squeeze of lemon,
and just enough olive oil to activate the compendium of flavors.*

HEAT SCALE: *mild*
BEST USE: *fresh or canned*

1-1¼ cups extra-virgin olive oil
8 large corno di toro peppers,
    seeded and sliced in half
    lengthwise or left whole
1 teaspoon fine sea salt
½ teaspoon freshly ground white
    pepper
2 tablespoons balsamic vinegar
3 cloves garlic, sliced
1 lemon, thinly sliced

In a large frying pan, heat ¼ cup of the oil over medium heat. Sauté the peppers 10-15 minutes, or until they begin to get tender. Remove the peppers from the heat and set aside.

In a small saucepan, warm the remaining oil over low heat. Add the salt, white pepper, and vinegar, blending with a whisk. Cook 20 minutes after the mixture boils.

If serving immediately, transfer the peppers to a serving dish along with the garlic and lemon slices. Pour the oil mixture over the peppers.

If canning, pack the peppers, then garlic, then lemon slices into hot, sterilized pint jars. Pour the oil mixture over the peppers, leaving ¼-inch headspace. Screw the lids and rings tightly on the jars, and process 10 minutes in a boiling-water bath. Remove the jars from the water and let stand in a draft-free area until the lids have popped.

Yields 2 pints

METRIC CONVERSIONS

Dry Weights

U.S. Measurements	Metric Equivalents
¼ ounce	7 grams
⅓ ounce	10 grams
½ ounce	14 grams
1 ounce	28 grams
1½ ounces	42 grams
1¾ ounces	50 grams
2 ounces	57 grams
3 ounces	85 grams
3½ ounces	100 grams
4 ounces (¼ pound)	114 grams
6 ounces	170 grams
8 ounces (½ pound)	227 grams
9 ounces	250 grams
16 ounces (1 pound)	464 grams

Liquid Weights

U.S. Measurements	Metric Equivalents
¼ teaspoon	1.23 ml
½ teaspoon	2.5 ml
¾ teaspoon	3.7 ml
1 teaspoon	5 ml
1 dessertspoon	10 ml
1 tablespoon (3 teaspoons)	15 ml
2 tablespoons (1 ounce)	30 ml
¼ cup	60 ml
⅓ cup	80 ml
½ cup	120 ml
⅔ cup	160 ml
¾ cup	180 ml
1 cup (8 ounces)	240 ml
2 cups (1 pint)	480 ml
3 cups	720 ml
4 cups (1 quart)	1 liter
4 quarts (1 gallon)	3¾ liters

Length

U.S. Measurements	Metric Equivalents
⅛ inch	3 mm
¼ inch	6 mm
⅜ inch	1 cm
½ inch	1.2 cm
1 inch	2.5 cm
¾ inch	2 cm
1¼ inches	3.1 cm
1½ inches	3.7 cm
2 inches	5 cm
3 inches	7.5 cm
4 inches	10 cm
5 inches	12.5 cm

Temperatures

Fahrenheit	Celsius (Centigrade)
32°F (water freezes)	0°C
200°F	95°C
212°F (water boils)	100°C
250°F	120°C
275°F	135°C
300°F (slow oven)	150°C
325°F	160°C
350°F (moderate oven)	175°C
375°F	190°C
400°F (hot oven)	205°C
425°F	220°C
450°F (very hot oven)	230°C
475°F	245°C
500°F (extremely hot oven)	260°C

SOURCES

Bella Cucina Artful Food
Bellissima! Inc.
5579 Peachtree Rd.
Atlanta, GA 30341
Phone: (770) 452-1819
Fax: (770) 452-1724

*Company specializes in artfully
packaged products such as preserved
lemons, cabernet vinegar, and
extra-virgin olive oil. Free product
information.*

Cheese Importers
33 South Pratt Parkway
Longmont, CO 80501-1717
Phone: (303) 443-4444
Fax: (303) 443-4492

*Wholesaler specializes in cheeses,
pepper condiments, and specialty
items such as textiles and kitchenware
from around the world. Open to the
public. Free product information.*

George W. Park Seed Company
Cokesbury Road
Greenwood, SC 29467-0001
Phone: (800) 845-3369
Fax: (864) 941-4206

*An all-purpose gardening supply com-
pany that offers seeds for vegetables,
fruits, herbs, and flowers as well as
small garden equipment. Free catalog.*

Joe's Vegetables
P.O. Box 2494
Hollister, CA 95024
Phone: (408) 636-3224
Fax: (408) 636-3226

*Organic wholesaler of vegetables,
fruits, and herbs.*

Johnny's Selected Seeds
Foss Hill Road
Albion, ME 04910-9731
Phone: (207) 437-4301
Fax: (207) 437-4301

*An all-purpose garden supplier that
offers a good variety of seeds for
vegetables, flowers (including edible
flowers), and herbs. Free catalog.*

The Pepper Gal
10536 119th Ave.
North Largo, FL 33543
Phone: (954) 537-5540
Fax: (954) 566-2208

*A seed source for sweet, hot, heir-
loom, and ornamental peppers. The
comprehensive product list is updated
and revised regularly. Send a self-
addressed stamped envelope for a free
pepper list and cookbook list.*

Pope Produce
3097 Road T
Wiggins, CO 80654
Phone: (970) 483-7839
Fax: (970) 483-7211

*Supplier of a wide variety of sweet
peppers, chiles, and melons.*

Sandy Mush Nursery
Rt. 2 Surrett Cove Rd.
Leicester, NC 28748
Phone: (704) 683-2014

*Seed and plant supplier with a
comprehensive array of herbs and
gourmet vegetables, including
hard-to-find varieties.*

Shepherd's Garden Seeds
30 Irene Street
Torrington, CT 06790-6627
Phone: (408) 335-6910

*Mail-order seed supplier of a wide
variety of vegetables and herbs. The
catalog includes gardener's tools as
well as recipes.*

**Tomato Growers Supply
Company**
P.O. Box 2237
Fort Myers, FL 33902
Phone: (941) 768-1119
Fax: (941) 768-3476

*Mail-order seed company offers
122 kinds of peppers and more
than 300 varieties of tomatoes.
Free catalog.*

Trout Lake Farm®
149 Little Mountain Road
Trout Lake, WA 98650
Phone: (509) 395-2025
Fax: (509) 395-2645

*A certified grower and processor of
organic herbs that cultivates medicinal
beverage and culinary herbs. Dried
spices include paprika, cayenne, and
chili powder.*

BIBLIOGRAPHY

Andrews, Jean. *Peppers*. Austin, Tex.: University of Texas Press, 1995.

Barrett, Judith. *From an Italian Garden*. New York: Macmillan Publishing Company, 1992.

Brissendan, Rosemary. *Asia's Undiscovered Cuisine*. New York: Pantheon Books, 1970.

Chioffi, Nancy, and Gretchen Mead. *Keeping the Harvest*. Pownal, Vt.: Storey Communications, 1991.

Chun, Lee To. *Chinese Cooking*. New York: Garland Books, 1973.

Dent, Huntley. *The Feast of Santa Fe: Cooking of the American Southwest*. New York: Simon & Schuster, 1985.

DeWitt, Dave, and Nancy Gerlach. *The Whole Chile Pepper Book*. Boston: Little Brown & Company, 1990.

DeWitt, Dave, and Paul W. Bosland. *The Pepper Garden*. Berkeley, Calif: Ten Speed Press, 1993.

Foster, Nelson, and Linda S. Cordell, eds. *Chilies to Chocolate*. Tucson, Ariz.: The University of Arizona Press, 1992.

Foster, Steven. *Herbal Renaissance*. Rev. ed. of *Herbal Bounty!*. Salt Lake City, Utah: Gibbs Smith Publisher, 1993.

Garzoni, Giovanna. *Florentines: A Tuscan Feast*. London: Pavillon Books Ltd., 1992.

Gordon, Lesley. *A Country Herbal*. New York: Mayflower Books, 1980.

Hazan, Marcella. *Essentials of Classic Italian Cooking*. New York: Knopf, 1992.

Hupping, Carol, and the staff at the Rodale Food Center. *Stocking Up*. New York, Simon & Schuster, 1986.

Kasper, Lynn. *The Splendid Table*. New York: William Morrow & Company, 1992.

Kennedy, Diana. *The Tortilla Book*. New York: Harper & Row, 1975.

——————. *The Cuisines of Mexico*. New York: Harper & Row, 1972.

Loha-Unchit, Kasma. *It Rains Fishes*. Rohnert Park, Calif: Pomegranate Artbooks, 1994.

McIlhenny, Paul, and Barbara Hunter. *The Tabasco Cookbook*. New York: Clarkson Potter, 1993.

Naj, Amal. *Peppers: A Story of Hot Pursuits*. New York: Knopf, 1992.

Ogden, Ellen, and Shepherd Ogden. *The Cook's Garden*. Emmaus, Pa.: The Rodale Press, 1989.

Rupp, Rebecca. *Blue Corn & Square Tomatoes*. Pownal, Vt.: Storey Communications, 1987.

Santin, Gino, and Anthony Blake. *La Cucina Veneziana*. New York: Prentice Hall Press, 1988.

Swahn, J. O. *The Lore of Spices*. New York: Crescent Books, 1991.

Yagley, Robert. *Poems from the Table*. New York: Barnes & Noble Books, 1995.

CREDITS

COVERS

Boyd Hagen

THE WORLD OF PEPPERS

p. 5, Derek Fell

p. 8, photography by Benko Photographics

A GALLERY OF PEPPERS

pgs. 16, 18, 22 (right), 23 (bottom left), 27 (bottom right), 31, 32, 35 (top right, bottom right), David Cavagnaro/SSE

pgs. 17, 20 (right), 23 (top left), 28 (right), 30 (left), 34, Chel Beeson

pgs. 19 (left), 20 (left), 34 (right), Shepherd's Garden Seeds

pgs. 19 (right), 21, 26 (bottom), 28 (left), 36 (left), Park Seed Company

pgs. 22 (left), 24, 25 (bottom), 27 (left), 30 (right), 33, Derek Fell

pgs. 23 (right), 25 (top), 29, courtesy of Johnny's Selected Seeds, Albion, Maine

p. 26 (top), © Virginia Twinam-Smith: Photo/Nats

pgs. 27 (top right), 35 (left), Boyd Hagen

p. 36 (right), © Liz Ball: Photo/Nats

HARVESTING AND STORING

pgs. 37, 39, 40, 41, 42, 43, 44, 45, 46, 47, 49, 50, photography by Benko Photographics

COOKING AND BAKING

pgs. 52, 54, 55, photography by Benko Photographics

RECIPES

pgs. 58, 67, 70, 76, 82, 88, 92, 97, 102, 107, 112, 116, 120, 125, 128, 133, 136, 141, 145, 149, Boyd Hagen

p. 153, photography by Benko Photographics

INDEX

INDEX

Associate Publisher: Helen Albert

Editorial Assistant: Cherilyn DeVries

Editor: Diane Sinitsky

Designer: Henry Roth

Layout Artist: Suzie Yannes

Illustrator: Rosalie Vaccaro

Typeface: Goudy

Paper: 70-lb. Somerset Gloss

Printer: Quebecor Printing/Hawkins, New Canton, Tennessee